# RHETORICAL TACTICS

*Esther M. Hamon*

*John Wiley & Sons, Inc., New York • London • Sydney • Toronto*

The text used on the cover
is from "Civil Disobedience" by Henry David Thoreau.

Copyright © 1972, by John Wiley & Sons, Inc.

All rights reserved. Published simultaneously in Canada.

No part of this book may be reproduced by any means, nor transmitted, nor translated into a machine language without the written permission of the publisher.

Library of Congress Catalogue Card Number: 77-177883

ISBN 0-471-34730-2

Printed in the United States of America.

10 9 8 7 6 5 4 3 2 1

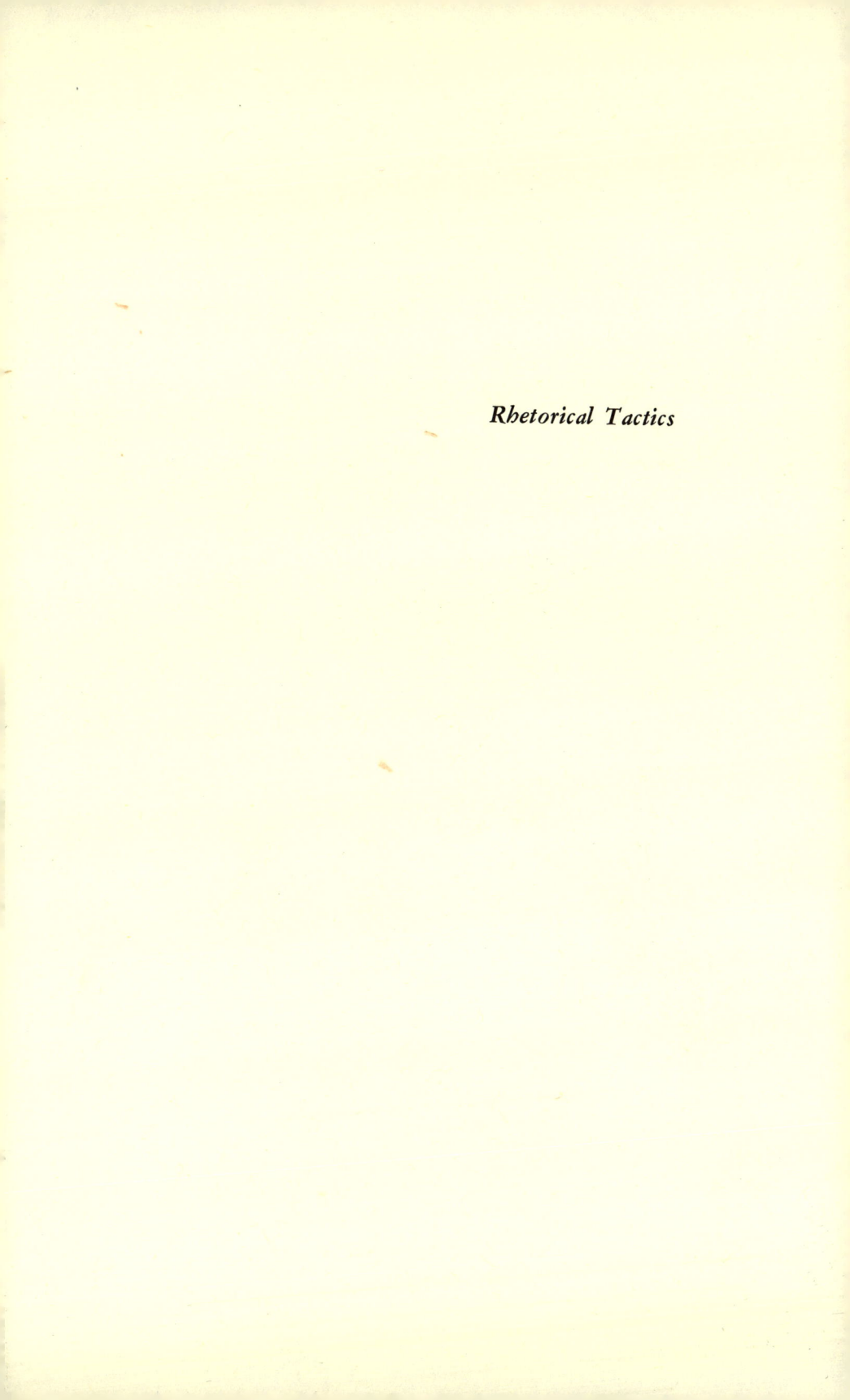

*Rhetorical Tactics*

# *PREFACE*

So you hate English and detest composition and have probably been led to believe that if you had just worked harder or paid more attention to instruction or learned the parts of speech all would be different. Don't you believe it! Your present attitude is, almost always, the direct result of our educational system. Nearly all of you began as enthusiastic first-graders, delighted to make up stories, eager to learn how to put your ideas on paper, but by grade 5, or maybe even earlier, the red ink corrections, the spelling drill, the nagging about punctuation killed this enthusiasm. From then on writing was drudgery. Of course, your teachers were not entirely to blame. Since a study of composition was but a small part of their training, they clung to textbooks and rules like a drowning man to his life-preserver. And, when the able teacher did want to help the individual, the heavy teaching load often prevented it.

You might have made up for this handicap by extensive reading. But Dick and Jane and their beloved Spot convinced you, perhaps, that books were stupid and not worth reading. Or you did not respond to this visual method of instruction and never learned to read well. Thus the benefits gained from the observation of professional writing, a satisfactory way to absorb the art of composition, were denied you.

Of course, if other methods had been used earlier, if your pleasure in reading and writing had been fostered, there would be no need for this text. Although there are changes for the better, this dreary situation still exists. Under these circumstances, you can do as my students and I did and go back to rhetoric, not the rhetoric of rules and mechanics, but the rhetoric which has come down to us from the days of ancient Greece. Stated as simply as possible, this rhetoric is the art of persuasion.

Rhetorical tactics, therefore, are those tactics or strategies which enable you to persuade the reader to accept your ideas. Naturally one expects changes to occur over the centuries, but when the changes went so far astray as they have done, perhaps it is wise to go back to its beginning and see what these Greek and Roman teachers did.

Those instructors began with a step-by-step process, until finally the student composed a whole composition. So, too, this book starts with small pieces: the word, the sentence, the paragraph. Those early teachers were practical men, but they also understood human nature. They believed that each student was more likely to succeed in more difficult writing if he had the confidence which comes from success in doing simpler pieces of composition first.

Since those methods of long ago are still useful, they provide much of the subject matter of this text. In discussing them I have used the names of those teachers and their terms, but this should not be too puzzling. As time goes on, such terminology becomes familiar.

Just as all of his education, his observations, and his experiences provided subject matter for the student of the past, so do you have a reservoir of knowledge to use today. Everyone, I believe, has a wealth of material for composition but, like the sugar maple, it has to be tapped. The short exercises help to do this.

While the readings included may suggest ideas for longer compositions, you will still need to draw upon your own experience in formulating ideas, quite possible as many of these prose pieces deal with modern problems. Discussion, both in and out of class, is urged as an introduction to the writing itself. This aids in clarifying the perception of a problem; in the oral give and take of discussion you learn where you stand on a subject, whether for or against. Persuasive composition demands commitment to one's views.

There are no chapters on spelling, punctuation, and usage. In my experience students who write to persuade make fewer errors. The very person who sprinkled in commas to satisfy his teacher uses the comma correctly if its absence would cause the reader to misinterpret his idea. Spelling may have been a problem, but dictionaries are more frequently used when persuasion is important. Those who used to say "Well, you just didn't understand what I meant" when a muddy sentence was called to their attention began to realize this was the result of a vague idea of where they stood. Once a definite stand is taken, muddy sentences disappear.

No, you won't write perfect compositions, but this book is written with the intention of convincing you that you will receive satisfaction in becoming a competent workman. Not every man becomes a master plumber; many learn to stop a leaky faucet.

Finally, you must realize that composition is not divorced from thinking. Besides giving you some competency in putting your own ideas on paper, this kind of study should prevent your being taken in by the false rhetoric that is a part of your world.

*Esther M. Hamon*

# CONTENTS

1  Introduction to Rhetoric   1

2  The Nature of Words: the Smallest Unit in a Composition   11

3  The Sentence: a Flexible Structure   27

4  The Paragraph: Making an Idea Clear to the Reader   45

5  The Proposition: the Thesis Statement the Writer Must Prove   54

6  The Appeals: Three Ways to Persuade the Reader   63

7  The Topics: Finding Out What You Know about a Subject   78

8  Three Kinds of Rhetorical Discourse   90

9  The Whole Composition: Each Part of the Plan for the Whole   97

10  The Entire Composition: Joining All the Parts Together   115

11  Style: As It Relates to Both Writer and Reader   131

12  Reading for Ideas: Looking for a Subject   140

   Index   173

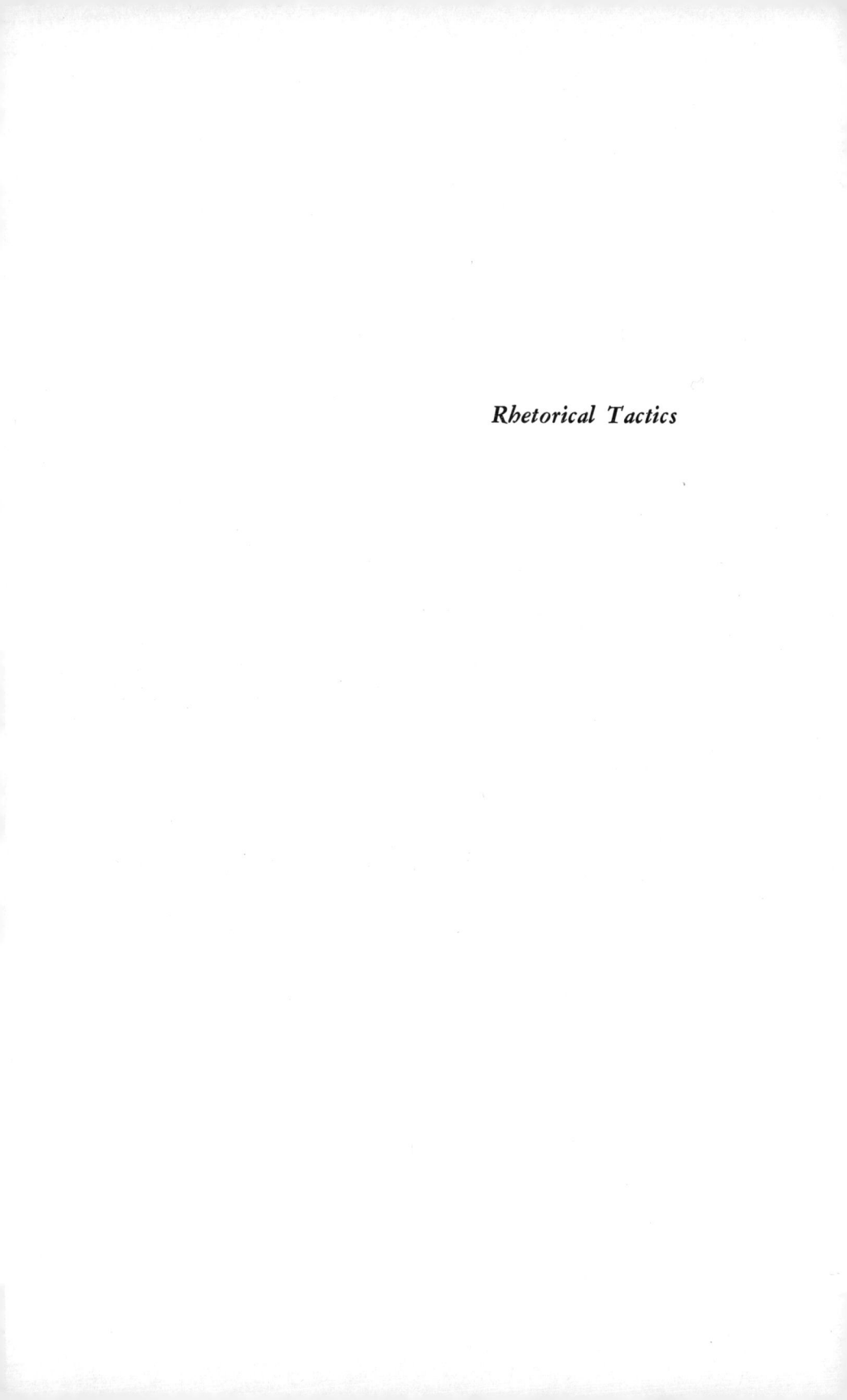

*Rhetorical Tactics*

CHAPTER ONE

# INTRODUCTION TO RHETORIC

Writing, if by that we mean making the configurations, the forms, we call words, is a skill many individuals have learned, though modern handwriting lacks the elaborateness of the eighteenth-century style, with its whorls and curlicues, or the flowing brushstrokes of Chinese calligraphy or handwriting. But writing as composing is different and more difficult. It demands thought, a collection of facts or ideas about a subject, finally culminating in the choice of topic, really the particular attitude adapted toward the subject, and then a utilization of these facts or ideas to prove the validity of the topic.

That sounds like a very formal way of describing a common action in our daily life, where we are always weighing pros and cons and then making choices, a hamburger or a grilled-cheese sandwich for example. But suppose we take a different kind of choice, the loss of a recreation area for a new highway. Can you toss off a flippant yes or no to this? If not, what facts can you find to help you decide which is really needed and, once having decided, can you urge your point of view persuasively?

In this era of oral report—TV, radio, films, and tapes—students may feel that learning to write is unnecessary, that every idea can be expressed orally. Yet the story told by H. Rap Brown in his political autobiography *Die, Nigger, Die!* denies this.

The son comes to the father and says, "You told me that the lion was the king of the jungle. Yet in every story I read, the man always beats the lion. Why is that?"

The father looks at the son and says, "Son, the story will always end the same until the lion learns how to write."[1]

[1] H. Rap Brown, *Die, Nigger, Die!* (New York: The Dial Press, Inc., 1969), p. 67.

**2  RHETORICAL TACTICS**

Now we might interpret this story as meaning that man is superior because writing meant he could keep and pass on much knowledge. But the true meaning, I feel, is that expressed by Levi-Strauss, the anthropologist, on the subject of writing. The primary result of this art to man, as he views it, was the building of cities and of empires, of a political system with varying castes and classes. To him writing seems "to favor rather the exploitation than the enlightenment of mankind."[2] He even suggests that the nineteenth-century struggle against illiteracy was, really, to bolster the power of authority, for when everyone can read laws, a person can't plead ignorance of them.

Thus the art of writing has given men a better chance in their society. Ability to express our ideas clearly and objectively may also aid us in judging the writing of others, understanding writing that is worthy and that calculated just to frighten or to fool us.

Perhaps we can best exemplify or show the basic training for this kind of writing by observing the *judoka* (judo player), his hands firmly grasping his opponent's *gi* (tunic to us), trying to find the proper hold which will enable him to throw his adversary. So, too, the writer must jockey for position, finding the particular way to approach his subject. His is not the physical combat of judo, but a kind of mental conflict in which he tries to find the best way to persuade the reader of the value or truth of his point of view.

But while the *judoka* spent much time earlier learning how to fall, for not everyone finds the successful grip, while he learned the ways in which an opponent could be thrown, our student writer often neglects the basic training needed for composition.

Perhaps this is not entirely the fault of the students nor of their teachers. For over the last century and at least part of this one, the firm foundation of composition was forgotten. Again, to return to our judo comparison, it would seem that if our textbooks and teachers (for after all they learned from the same kind of textbooks) had been teaching judo, they would have concentrated upon the costume, the posture, the exact angle of the polite bow preceding combat, and concentrated none at all upon the falls or throws which are the essence or core of judo.

---

[2] Claude Levi-Strauss, *Tristes Tropiques,* translated by John Russell (New York: Criterion Books, 1961), p. 292.

Now, however, in the hope that as students of composition we may learn something of the art of writing, this book will center its attention upon the field of rhetoric. For just as judo is an ancient Eastern art so is rhetoric an ancient Western one. And just as the art of combat, or jujitsu, became a sport called judo, so down the centuries rhetoric, the art of persuasion, became known as composition.

It all started more than two thousand years ago, although it wasn't until the second quarter of the fifth century B.C. that we have any particular set of rules to describe or teach this art. According to the story there was a tyrant in Sicily who confiscated the property of many citizens, resulting, of course, in legal argument when he was finally overthrown. A man named Corax, observing the cases in court, noticed that the speeches for those who won the cases consisted of four parts: introduction, proposition (This land should belong to me), the argument, and the conclusion.

Thus began the attention to the form of the speech, for in those days before printing, much was oral, not written communication. Greece studied this art; so did Rome. Schools of rhetoric spread, although some were much criticized by the philosopher Plato, who felt that some of the teachers were unethical.

The situation was similar to that in our own country at the end of World War II. As soon as the G.I. Bill passed, assuring the returning veteran of financial aid for education, quack schools and correspondence courses began, much more interested in the G.I.'s money than in his education. So were some schools of rhetoric fond of cash.

Plato assumed that rhetorical, that is, composition, techniques could persuade people that what was false was true and what was true, false. There was probably some reason for his views since another Greek, the playwright Aristophanes, in his play *The Clouds,* has the father of a spendthrift son urging the young man to go to a school of rhetoric where he could learn this art of persuasion so well that he could get out of paying his creditors.

Plato's criticism was not quite fair to all the teachers of rhetoric and their schools, for a teacher like Isocrates believed that a good rhetorician had to be a good man, not in the goody-goody sense, but good in that he thought deeply, studied the problem, had the welfare of his audience at heart. Plato accepted this, but he also insisted that such a man should find out the truth before he could discuss a question.

## 4 RHETORICAL TACTICS

Once a man had discovered the truth, Plato argued, then he was ready to discuss the proposition, the statement he would make about his subject.

But another philosopher and teacher disputed this. Perhaps to prove the arguments of Plato were incorrect, Aristotle produced the *Art of Rhetoric*. Men, in Aristotle's opinion, often could not argue from a knowledge of truth, since no one may really know it. All a man can do is to persuade people that his ideas offer the best course of action. Until Columbus proved the world was round, there could be debate about it; and once being shown that the world was indeed round, there could be no further argument concerning it.

In my childhood, for example, no one considered reaching the moon. We were more likely to consider its romantic quality than its craters. Jules Verne, the early author of what we now call space-fiction, could write *From the Earth to the Moon,* but this was just a fantastic story to his readers. Not until technology reached a stage where reaching the moon became possible did man debate whether or not to do so. Then it became more of an argument over purpose and finances.

Almost all the arguments of society are based upon this theory of probability, the men who argue proposing that their plan of action is the best. The Greeks could argue about the Persians; Athens about its long and devastating war; and modern man about his boundaries, his finances, and his welfare. There always seem to be two sides to each question, and whoever presents the best argument may win. Plato urged that speakers know the truth. Aristotle more practically asked, "How can they?"

History will probably show that, like Athens, we have suffered from a prolonged war. To a generation aware of the failure to oppose Hitler's early moves, action seemed warranted in Vietnam. Others saw it as a different situation. Thus there was argument. As Aristotle reasoned, man can only deliberate and try to forecast the best of probable actions. Thus, this kind of persuasive speech came to be known as the deliberative.

Another kind, usually a speech in honor of some person or event, such as the Gettysburg address, was called a ceremonial speech. A third, the speeches of the law court, was called the forensic; the speeches of the defense and of prosecuting attorneys in our courts today still cling to the Aristotelian pattern.

All of Aristotle's ideas were adapted by the Romans and, when Latin was still a popular subject in our schools, all Latin scholars studied the orations of Cicero, who not only studied the art but, as a statesman, practiced it. Despite Cicero's interest in rhetoric, perhaps Quintilian, a Roman teacher, was of greater help to students of rhetoric, but as the years went on there were, as usual, changes. No longer was rhetoric just a part of Greek and Roman education. It spread over the continent of Europe, continuing through what historians call the Middle Ages and the Renaissance. In 1504 we find Erasmus, the most influential rhetorician on the Continent, coming to England, where he set the pattern for rhetorical training in the schools, particularly in St. Paul's school, founded at that time. Some scholars kept to the traditional forms they had always used; others, thinking the subject too broad divided it, putting logic or reason in one area, and style or how a thing was said in another.

As time went on, rhetoric was really almost a lost art. Our texts spoke of narration, description, exposition, and argument as separate areas, although all of these might be used in one rhetorical presentation. Style, as shown in the multiplicity or great number of figures of speech in Shakespeare's day, became little more than correct usage, correct in the eyes of the grammarian, the scholar who studied the grammar of a language, but not always the speech of the people themselves.

This gradual disintegration or breaking apart was still common at the beginning of the twentieth century. Then, in the 1920s, there began a revival of rhetoric, the art of persuasion. Perhaps the times were becoming more troublesome, for, as we go back through our history, we find that times of social unrest called for the rhetorical speeches. We find them in the *Federalist* papers (those papers urging the adoption of the U.S. Constitution), the speeches of Thomas Paine; we find them in practically perfect classical form in the speeches of Frederick Douglass as he argued for freedom for his people; and again in times of war or in times of social strife that affect our country today.

There is, however, as I write this at the beginning of the 1970s, a kind of rhetoric that differs from that of the past. Slogans, signs, and parades appear as well as persuasive articles and speeches. While one article may still discuss and urge an anti-pollution campaign, a Pete Seeger sings a ballad about the pollution of the Hudson River. But song or demonstration is, like the speeches of Cicero, persuasive in purpose.

Unfortunately, however, almost the greatest use of rhetoric in recent decades has been in advertising. Here, all too much of it has followed the pattern of rhetoric which Plato detested, the kind which swayed people to accept false conclusions. If we are not to be dominated or overwhelmed by rhetoric, that is, persuasion used in the wrong way, if we are to learn to use it for our benefit, we need to study its principles. That is what this text is all about.

We need to know the principles or rules of this art. We may not, like the judo master, win a black belt; we may not, like the good novelist, win a Nobel prize; we can win the satisfaction of presenting our ideas concisely, logically, and clearly. Even if we do not put our ideas on paper in the form of writing, the principles of rhetoric can help us to think more clearly and make better decisions, something which is required of all of us. Just as the experienced judoka may find his knowledge of the art useful in saving him from a harmful fall rather than helping him in combat, so we find rhetoric helpful in our daily lives.

This brings us to the problem of learning any new art, that of vocabulary, the words we use in discussing the art itself. There has been an idea that textbooks should not use words that may not be in the vocabulary of the boy or girl in that particular grade. This was rather silly, for what author truly knows the vocabulary of the reader? Besides, how can we increase our store of words if new words are never met? It all reminds me of the old jingle:

> "Mother, may I go out to swim?"
> "Yes, my darling daughter.
> Hang your clothes on the hickory limb,
> But don't go near the water."

It is as if the teacher of judo told all boys not to learn the art until they were really fully-grown.

Therefore, in this text I shall use the vocabulary needed for describing the art of rhetoric. I shall refer to these strange names like Aristotle, Isocrates, Quintilian, or Erasmus because it only seems fair to give credit to the authors of exercises which can help us learn to write. They should not be considered as names for quizzes. It is as easy to pick up the terms for composition or rhetoric as it is to learn those for any new sport.

*Introduction to Rhetoric* 7

But you won't bother with terms or basic steps if you are sure that composition is just the school's game, and it often has been. You should see composition as a way of expressing and defending your own ideas, as well as evaluating and attacking, when necessary, the ideas of others.

Here is a sample of composition, a speech by Mr. Jim Drake,[3] Administrative Assistant of the United Farm Workers in Delano, California, and one of Cesar Chavez's chief assistants. He was asked to tell a group of teachers and educators working to improve the training of elementary teachers about the educational situation in his area. Although its purpose is explanatory, his speech is persuasive. He could have refused the invitation to speak, saying this was not his field. Instead he convinced this group of the problem they faced. Could you do as well for your community?

I've been perplexed all day; I can't figure out what I'm doing here, because for the Farm Worker's Union, which is made up predominantly of Mexican-Americans and Filipino-Americans and black Americans and poor white Americans in the San Joaquin Valley of California, the whole education system is just a joke; we don't even talk about it; we just laugh. So we don't even talk about getting control of school boards or participating in decision-making processes that would affect farm workers. I haven't even thought of it until today.

I think the major reason is basically that farm workers can't vote. There are a number of reasons why farm workers can't vote. A lot of them are Mexican citizens; that makes it a little difficult to vote, in this country anyway. But they have children here, and their children go to school here. If they're not Mexican citizens and international migrants, then they're migrants across county and state lines and they're not in one county long enough to register to vote. So we've had very bad experiences with schools and I think schools have had bad experience with farm workers. There are a lot of programs developed for farm workers' kids, and they're all just so many farces.

I think the basic reason is that our society has a school system which is developed in such a way that it's meant to provide a commodity for the market—the well-rounded mediocrity that goes to college and then fits into the

---

[3] U.S. Office of Education, "A Pride of Lions," Fourth National Conference, Tri-University Project in Elementary Education, September 19–20, 1968, Minneapolis, Minn.

upper echelons of our society that control the little people down here. So we have Columbia University preparing for a war this year over the sources of their money and the sources of their power. And we have the University of California at Davis preparing for a war this year, because for years and years they've turned out machines and ideas and systems for agriculturalists in California, which have amassed huge amounts of money for a very small five per cent of the farm workers in the state.

Now that a union has come along and decided that it's going to help farm workers and they are developing their own ideas and own plans for grasping a little bit of that power that we've just been talking about, the growers go to the Giannini Foundation and to Emperor Reagan and ask that these peasants down here be put back in their place, which is supposed to be slavery; the way to cut off this machine which they're developing, this power machine, is with another machine—mechanize them out of business, plow them under. So they come up with the mechanical grape picker; they come up with the mechanical almond shaker—whoever thought of shaking almonds out of the tree with a machine? They come up with a machine that blocks sugar beets so that they won't need Mexicans anymore—that beautiful breed that the growers always talked about, built short and close to the ground so that they can use a short handled hoe. They won't be needed anymore, they won't have a need for a union or any reason to have any power. And all of this is a result of our education system.

But I don't want to blame the education system alone, because the education system is merely the cogs of the machine by which we police the whole world and the system by which we control the world, the system by which we are careful to keep our supremacy on this globe. I didn't used to believe this until I saw what happened in Chicago; I'm kind of a conservative guy anyway. And my father's a teacher, my sister is a teacher. I don't talk to them anymore.

Some of you shake your heads: I don't know if you're shaking your heads because you're sorry it's that way or because you don't agree with me. I didn't used to think it was true but I believe it now; I believe it because I've been involved for six years with a ragged bunch of farm workers who are trying to form a union, and almost every goddamn weapon that this government has, has been used to keep them from having it. For instance, say they strike within two hundred miles of the Mexican border: two thousand workers leave the field and they leave the complete area; the grapes are there, and you've pulled your power play. The government says, "Well, we're not sure about the law, whether or not Mexicans from across the border can come and break strikes, but we'll have to take it to the Supreme Court and decide. Meantime, we'll have to employ them because it has to be settled that way." So the strike is broken and the grapes are harvested. What's the use of building power if the government is going to use its ability to allow strike breakers to come across the border?

. . . . .

. . . But more and more as we deal with the local school board system and the way that the local school board in rural America deals with conflict in its community, I'm becoming convinced that the school system is the hatchery for all those big roosters that go around crowing all over the country, and that it's through the hatchery system that we incubate them and we send them up to the university, where they become the C.I.A. of the world, that we're bogged down in a fantastically impossible situation. Therefore, if the local teacher who wants to do something about it, he stands up and says something about it, he becomes just a bloody mess, because he is a nonentity.

In Delano, the school board is made up of growers and if the teachers wanted to stand up and say, "Cesar Chavez's kids, all eight of them, have the right to wear *huelga* buttons to school that say that they believe in what their father is working for," the board, made up of growers, would just can them like that. So they don't say anything.

We talked about this in our discussion group and I commiserated a little bit. It just seems to me that if teachers think that anything that I'm saying has any validity, and if they think it is true that our society is being nursemaided by the school system, then they had better organize and they had better make coalitions—and it had better not be with growers if you want to make any changes for the better. It ought to be with poor people, it ought to be with black people, it ought to be with the students—the right students —the *left* students. And I think, finally, that the students who are planning on being teachers ought to spend some time in the communities where they're going to teach, looking at things, seeing what's going on, before they get out there. And then they're going to be able to communicate with those other students in the university.

I just want to say that in three years of strike in Delano, we've had student social workers, we've had student dental technicians and student nurses, we've had guys that are planning to be doctors, we've had seminary students, historians, almost every kind of student under the sun, come to Delano to talk to us and see what the problem of the farm worker trying to get in the union is; *but we haven't had one goddamn student teacher come.* I don't know if they don't know where Delano is or they don't read the newspapers or what, but they're sure welcome. We hope they come.

*Exercise* 1

Give a situation about which you could speak if you were asked. Are you prepared to do so? If you are, why do you think you could persuade your audience? If you are not, what stands in the way? How could you prepare yourself for giving such a speech if you feel unprepared now?

CHAPTER TWO

# THE NATURE OF WORDS: THE SMALLEST UNIT IN A COMPOSITION

The student of judo learns that for any action there is a reaction. If we substitute *word* for *action* this rule also applies to composition. For words, like actions, create a reaction on the part of the hearer or reader. But while the well-trained *judoka,* through experience, may be able to interpret his or his opponent's reaction to certain motions or forces, the interpretations, translating or understanding, of words is more difficult. If a speaker or writer has had the same background as his listener or reader, he can, in a way, sense the reaction. In an age when a society was limited in size, when quite similar ideas and customs were held by the whole group, a speaker could be quite sure of how to appeal to the group and what their reaction would be. Virgil could be quite sure when he wrote the *Aeneid,* a narrative poem from the days of Rome, that his readers would not blame the hero Aeneas for deserting Dido the Queen. After all, the fate of Aeneas was to found Rome and all was forgiven for that. The Victorians accepted Tennyson's version of the "gallant six hundred" who died before the Russian cannon at Balaclava during the Crimean War. Then they were gallant. Today we wonder what fool of a commander could think that cavalry equals cannons. For today is different. Printing and mass communications bring the most diverse or different groups into the speaker's or writer's range. But this doesn't mean he is in tune with all of that mass audience. He may be able to sense the feelings of many people but not all of them.

We may live in one country, but even so, cultures differ. This isn't apparent when we first learn words, a process which takes place very early indeed. Listen to the babblings of a young child. He is experimenting with the sounds he hears. If he isn't deaf, he very soon learns to imitate the language of those about him. His speech is the language of his family. As he grows older he absorbs the words of his play companions, then of school, then of his job.

One of our realizations about language is that men have a variety of dialects. We use speech much like dress, attiring ourselves or fitting our speech to the occasion. Changing our dress does not mean discarding the old; we just add a new piece of wearing apparel to our wardrobe. We do the same in our speech. And from our dialects we choose the one which is suited to the occasion. Our problem lies, probably, in acquiring the dialects we need or in recognizing the reactions that certain dialects may call forth. Profanity to you may be a part of everyday speech for me, but if I know you feel this way I'll censor my speech in talking to you.

Our old composition texts have really led us astray. They have talked of specific words, concrete and abstract nouns, descriptive words, words which appeal to the senses, taught that the meaning for a word is a dictionary definition (though it may vary in different contexts—fair day and fair play), that all words have synonyms or comparable meanings, and that a standard dialect use of the word gives the same meaning to everyone and calls forth the same reaction.

Because texts and teachers have succeeded in giving the impression that there is a standard language, oral as well as written, people lack confidence in their ability to express themselves in words. If so much of their oral speech is wrong, they reason then that their writing is sure to be wrong. As a result, I know many of you couldn't care less about composition, but it seems downright stupid to have free speech as part of the Bill of Rights if only a few can profit by it. Remember that each of you has a fairly extensive but diversified vocabulary, that if you honestly try to make your ideas clear to your reader, you can probably do it.

Some of us as teachers have learned that all children can express themselves; in fact this is the primary topic of Herbert Kohl's book, *36 Children*. Our older pupils can do this too if—and this is the problem —they are interested in the subject and if they are not first given a thousand and one rules about how an idea must be said. My experience has taught me that a person who wants to express an idea can. Again, to return to judo, the teacher doesn't just talk about the art; he lets his

## The Nature of Words: The Smallest Unit in a Composition 13

pupils use their muscles and their bodies. Or take basketball. Imagine the results if coaches just talked about how to dribble a ball and never let the players on the floor until game time. So the beginning writer needs less advice and more chance to write and to write about what he knows.

You do, however, need to consider your words and the way they and the examples you choose will affect your reader. In ancient Greece where people argued their own cases in court, individuals learned very quickly to consider how the group would react to what they said.

It may have been this idea which led George Orwell to write his "Politics and the English Language,"[1] since he recognized that jargon can hamper relationships between countries as well as people. He calls our attention to the word *democracy* and says:

> It is almost universally felt that when we call a country democratic we are praising it: consequently the defenders of every kind of regime claim that it is a democracy, and fear that they might have to stop using the word if it were tied down to any one meaning.

This leads, of course, to using words in a dishonest way.

Teachers as well as students must recognize that language is the person; language is our life, for language comes from life. In his speech to American scholars, Emerson[2] emphasized that this must be remembered:

> If it were only for a vocabulary, the scholar would be covetous of action. Life is our dictionary.... I learn immediately from any speaker how much he has already lived, through the poverty or splendor of his speech. Life lies behind us as the quarry from which we get tiles and copestones [New England was known for its rocky land] for the masonry of today. This is the way to learn grammar. Colleges and books only copy the language which the field and the work yard made.

This idea, that we get words from what we do and hear in our daily life, explains why I am sure that no student is wholly without

---

[1] George Orwell, *A Collection of Essays* (Garden City, N.Y.: Doubleday and Company, Inc., 1954), p. 169.

[2] Ralph Waldo Emerson, "The American Scholar," *Basic Selections from Emerson*, edited by Edward C. Lindeman (New York: New American Library, 1954), p. 111.

the vocabulary necessary for writing. Often, I think, our texts have implied that good writing must have a completely different set of words, that for even an ordinary occasion we must have more formal dress. In some instances this attitude has probably led the student into copying the wordy clauses and phrases Orwell calls jargon. In others it has left him feeling that he doesn't have the tools; therefore he can't write.

He can learn, but transferring the language of life to the written page is not a simple matter. The gestures, the half-sentences, the intonation or stress put on words to show feelings can't be shown in the written form. Neither can you always be sure of the audience. The story-teller of past ages knew his listeners. He knew their vocabulary. That isn't true today, with the result that Emerson's language of the work-a-day world often becomes a more standard English on the printed page. Yet, despite this, the writer does have freedom of choice. Our language has so many words, so many variations of meaning. But you have to choose the right word to get the right reaction. As George Romney learned when he was a candidate for the presidency, if his public attached a derogatory idea to the term "brainwash," then his possibility of becoming a candidate was weakened. He withdrew from the competition.

Here are five questions you can discuss about language.

1. Why do people often misunderstand each other even when using words they know?
2. Why may a word be a symbol of different meaning to different people?
3. In what way does a person's feelings and experiences have anything to do with the way he interprets a word's meaning?
4. Why are students often inclined to accept words which may appeal to them but which obscure meaning?
5. What part do words play in the thinking process?

In all the exercises in this chapter about words, keep these directions in mind.

1. Use your own experiences.
2. Examine your subject carefully for only in this way will you notice details which must be described.

3. Be very selective in your choice of words as you want them to appeal to the reader.

## A

The exercises which follow may seem very petty when applied to such an important topic as words, and the impression may have been given that there really can't be communication among men. Yet if communication is desirable, then one of the best ways to start is to do some simple exercises which depend upon the choice of words.

Remember the judo expert doesn't ever begin by competing with an opponent. Instead he spends hours learning how to fall correctly so that if he is thrown later he won't be hurt. Therefore, you must practice in order to achieve at least some measure of communication, for misunderstandings hurt too.

Think of the phrase "Black Power." To the person who is insecure or just advancing in material ways, it is like the term, "French Revolution," overthrowing a social group. To one who recognizes that in our society matters are determined politically as a rule, this means that blacks may be better able to solve their problems if they too can win political influence. Another term that has aroused fear is that of *socialism*. It can, of course, be of a totalitarian kind; it can also be a national measure for the good of many citizens. But call a measure "socialized" and many react unfavorably.

Some terms may arouse a favorable reaction. Free enterprise probably exited from the American scene years ago, yet the very citizen who is far from free in his job or his life generally will bellow about keeping *free enterprise*.

Slogans are catchy; they can be effective; they can also backfire, particularly when, with mass media, they spread so quickly.

*Exercise 1*

Make a list of words: (a) five words you remember learning as a child, (b) five words you learned from your friends, and (c) five words you learned at school or on the job.

*Exercise 2*

This may seem like a trivial exercise, particularly since it is solely for you, not for a grade. At first it will be more of a timetable. Then it becomes, or should become, an expression of what you think and feel. This is the basis for writing.

 a. Keep a journal for the next five or ten days. Jot down words or phrases (these need not be sentences) that will help you recall something you especially felt that day.

 b. Go over your journal to see how many of these recent experiences are connected to past ones.

 c. Compare, if you care to, your journal with others. See if your notes indicate to others any idea of the experience you had.

*Exercise 3*

List several comments you might hear from students concerning a school situation. Then judge them from the point of view of an administrator, a parent, a townsperson. Would they get the meaning the student gave them? What might be the problem?

*Exercise 4*

Here is a passage from the Bible, a verse from Ecclesiastes; *a* is as it appears in the King James version, *b* is the way George Orwell translated it into modern English.

Read both *a* and *b* and then tell, if you can, why a composition class I once had told me they preferred *b*, although, as they also confessed, they did not understand it. Why would Orwell, do you suppose, prefer the first?

 a. I returned and saw under the sun, that the race is not to the swift, nor the battle to the strong, neither yet bread to the wise, nor yet riches to men of understanding, nor yet favor to men of skill; but time and chance happeneth to them all.
 b. Objective consideration of contemporary phenomena compels the conclusion that success or failure in competitive activities exhibits no tendency to be commensurate with innate capacity, but that a considerable element of the unpredictable must invariably be taken into account.[3]

# B

Writing should make the reader feel that your experience is also his. Your words should stimulate his imagination so that he goes beyond sharing your experience into recalling his own feelings in a

---

[3] George Orwell, *A Collection of Essays* (Garden City, N.Y.: Doubleday and Company, Inc., 1954), p. 169.

recollection of similar experiences from his past. Although what happened to him may not have been exactly the same it probably aroused the same emotions or feelings. In one not very long sentence Ernest Hemingway convinced a student of mine that he was describing a fishing pool this student had seen. Hemingway wasn't, but the details he mentioned made my student picture his own experience so vividly he really felt it had been described.

Part of the problem in finding words to do this is not a lack of vocabulary but a lack of observation. A science teacher I know asked a group of people training to be teachers to do the kind of observation their pupils could do, keeping a notebook to record what happened each day in spring as the dead branches of winter came alive. And, day after day, the entries read "No change." But there was change. I watched a cherry tree branch outside my kitchen window. The tiny tight brown buds swelled a bit each day; the color of the brown was deeper, then lighter. Eventually there were blooms: first a tinge of pink peeping through, then a tight, slightly lighter-pink bud, and then the bloom, the entire blossom more white than pink. And finally, of course, bright red cherries. What really bothered me was that I had so frequently paid no attention myself to this evidence of approaching spring.

In my college days I had read Thoreau's *Walden,* an account of his life by Walden Pond. And I read, probably thoughtlessly, his account of the coming of spring, his description of the melting of ice in the pond, of the melting of ice and snow on the banks of the railroad tracks, of how the water begins to flow, taking the sandy soil with it. Yet I need not read *Walden* for this. I can watch the same process after a hard winter, see the ice melt, the water run into the gutters. All I need to do is to watch. And what we teachers need to do is to observe and to get our pupils to observe. Everyone has words to use, but no one can find words to describe what he has never really observed or never really listened to. Here is probably the cause of the "limited" vocabulary. It is limited, not because the person hasn't the words, but because he doesn't record all the observations he could make about an experience.

Read this paragraph from *The Invisible Man.* The author[4] could

---

[4] Ralph Ellison, *The Invisible Man* (New York: New American Library, 1968), p. 228.

have written: I bought a roasted yam, which reminded me of meals back home. But notice what he does with it.

> Then far down at the corner I saw an old man warming his hands against the sides of an odd-looking wagon, from which a stovepipe reeled off a thin spiral of smoke that drifted the odor of baking yams slowly to me, bringing a stab of swift nostalgia. I stopped as though struck by a shot, deeply inhaling, remembering, my mind surging back, back. At home we'd bake[d] them in the hot coals of the fireplace, had carried them cold to school for lunch, munched them secretly, squeezing the sweet pulp from the soft peel as we hid from behind the largest book, the World's Geography. Yes, and we'd loved them candied, or baked in a cobbler, deep-fat fried in a pocket of dough, or roasted with pork and glazed with the well-browned fat: had chewed them raw—yams—years ago. More yams than years ago though the time seemed endlessly expanded, stretched thin as the spiraling smoke beyond all recall.

I read this and add to it: the yam I forgot to pierce and which exploded in my oven; my early days at school and the candy wafers one boy passed around to those who sat near him; winter days in the city when I passed a chestnut vendor and bought a bag of roasted chestnuts. I can still recall their sweet nutty flavor. I am, as a result of Ellison's description, less of an outsider, more of a concerned reader.

These exercises should help you do what Ellison did, make the reader share the experience.

*Exercise* 1

What food or dish would make you feel as this author did? Write words or phrases describing it.

*Exercise* 2

The traffic light changes from red to green. Think of several words or phrases to describe the movement of the traffic.

*Exercise* 3

A person is said to be "old," but what does that mean to the reader? Is he old in voice, in movement, in appearance, in his ideas? Look carefully at an old person you know and list words or phrases that would make another person really understand what you meant by "old."

*Exercise* 4

If I write "On my way home from school I used to pass a foundry where I saw the workers carrying and pouring molten metal from large ladles," there isn't any quality of fear. Yet, I know that as a child I disliked going by that building but was too intrigued by the sight to hurry past. How could I say it to let someone else get the feeling I had? Should I describe the smell, for there was one of heat? Should I try to tell the color of the fiery metal? Could it be that the men themselves, stripped to the waist, bending as they carried their flaming scoops, silhouetted against the shadowy foundry walls, were the ones I feared?

Write a list of words or phrases describing a scene which used to frighten you.

*Exercise* 5

Here is the product of an author from Kenya, John Mbiti. English is his second language, but can you get his view of New York? Which of his expressions seem particularly effective?

### *New York Skyscrapers*[5]

The weak scattered rays of yellow sun
Peeped through the hazy tissues
That blanketed them with transparent wax;
And as the wrinkled rays closed the day,
Smoky chimneys of New York coughed
Looking down in bended towers
And vomited sad tears of dark smoke.

## C

Composition exercises have frequently urged the student to select words appealing to the senses: sight, sound, hearing, smelling, and feeling. Very little advice is given as to how this is to be done or that it usually can't be done without reliving in our mind the experience, and we often forget the experience because we have observed too little. To mean something to us we must have absorbed enough details to make us able to relive this experience.

---

[5] Gerald Moore and Ulli Beier, eds., *Modern Poetry From Africa* (Baltimore, Md.: Penguin African Library, 1966), p. 163.

Perhaps this is the talent of the poet. I say it is a fine day, but he tells me *how* it is fine. Certain odors, certain sights can call forth past incidents in your experience. Since many of the things which happen to you happen to others, a description which enables the reader to recall his experiences makes him a sympathetic reader. He is more willing to accept what you say.

What you may not have been told is that the remembered experience is vivid because the mind has noted all the sensory details surrounding it. Better advice for the beginning writer would be that old sign at railroad crossings: "Stop, look, and listen."

In the following exercises you will have a chance to experiment with ways to call forth these appeals to the senses.

*Exercise* 1

A good start is to sit down, close one's eyes and listen. Don't close your eyes in the middle of a busy crossing to listen, and if you do this in class the teacher will accuse you of going to sleep. Pretend you are a blind man standing on the curb. Is there a rustle which indicates the lights have changed? Do you hear a click as the lights change? Is there any building going on? Do you hear the sound of a cement-mixer? Listen. Then jot down words or phrases to tell what you hear.

*Exercise* 2

Now open your eyes and look at a downtown street. List all you can see. If there is a brick wall, don't just record that it is brick. Is it old or new brick, red or brown? Is the mortar new or is it crumbling? Is the pavement a dirty gray, black tar, pot-hole cement? Look!

*Exercise* 3

Can you feel? It is a hot, hot day. As you pass by a big brick building, do the bricks give off waves of heat? Do you feel perspiration coming out on your skin? As you pass a building does an opening door let forth a breeze from the air-conditioning within? Do your shoes seem too tight? Does your shirt or blouse scratch? How do you feel? Jot down words and phrases telling us this. Or you might be cold. How could you make us feel that?

*Exercise* 4

Perhaps, as air pollution continues, as gasoline fumes take over, our sense of smell will decrease, but at present we can still sense odors. Can you find words or phrases to make the person who is not with you, smell the odors you do? Can you make him think of odors he relates to certain places? For example, the smell of roasting coffee will always recall to me a hot Chicago summer. Each day the bus passed a building where coffee was being roasted and its odor on a humid day made the whole area one of coffee.

## D

Words often seem designed to call forth favorable or unfavorable reactions. This is why, as Orwell said, governments describe themselves as democratic, for people react favorably to this word. The fat woman prefers to be called plump; the skinny one to be called thin. A man won't lie, for that is wrong; but he will fib, a lesser evil. Considering that people are individuals, that their experiences may determine their feelings, it is difficult to be objective, either in reporting on incidents or in analyzing the reports of others. Your feelings, your past experiences often color what you say. Perhaps the following exercises may indicate this problem.

*Exercise* 1

A high school student has had an accident with his car. Give three words which each of these witnesses would use in court to describe this boy:
   *a.* The witness who thinks all teen-agers are irresponsible.
   *b.* The traffic officer
   *c.* The school counselor
   *d.* The boy's parent

*Exercise* 2

Mrs. H—— has been asked to give a reference for her baby-sitter. What two words might she use:
   *a.* if she liked the baby-sitter;
   *b.* if her child had not liked the baby-sitter?

*Exercise* 3

   Mr. A—— insists upon watching football on TV.
   Mrs. A—— thinks this a waste of time.
What three words might each use about a "bowl" game?

*Exercise* 4

The atmosphere is often determined by the verb of the sentence.
         The boy *walked* down the street, *crossed* the vacant
               lot, and *disappeared* into the building.

*a.* Change the underlined words to ones which suggest the boy is getting away from danger.

*b.* Change the words to suggest he is in a great hurry.

*c.* Change the words to suggest he is just enjoying a long walk on a spring day.

*Exercise 5*

Mrs. J—— is in her late fifties. Her hair isn't always combed neatly. She is five feet four and slightly overweight. She laughs a lot but is easily provoked. She is very cautious about spending and likes things in order.

List three words which give a favorable or unfavorable picture of Mrs. H——.

*Exercise 6*

Joe H—— wears a beard. His hair is somewhat long. He works hard but after work hangs about the street corner with friends.

List three words which give a favorable or unfavorable picture of Joe H——.

*Exercise 7*

A school paper announces that the home team "crushed" the opponent; but on a TV broadcast, reaching supporters of both teams, the announcer simply says that A won and B lost. Look at the sports accounts in newspapers and list words you find used in reporting on games.

*Exercise 8*

The "Romantic poets," often considered dull by high school students, were really rebels, revolting against the "age of reason" and urging writing which appealed to the senses. DeQuincy, an essayist, even recorded his dreams in "Confessions of an English Opium Eater." Try to describe an experience of yours which had a definitely sensory appeal. Try to make the reader feel it with you.

# E

Textbooks of journalism may tell the student to find other words for *said:* reply, state, assert, say, etc. An author may, like Kenneth Grahame in *Wind in the Willows*,[6] have the same verb but change the effect by the modifier he uses. Here are a few of his examples:

---

[6] Kenneth Grahame, *Wind in the Willows* (New York: Charles Scribner's Sons, 1965), pp 110–11.

"That's no good!" said the Rat *contemptuously*.
"Sit down there, Toad," said the Badger *kindly*, . . .
"That is very good news," said the Mole *gravely*.
"No!" he said a little *sullenly*, but *stoutly*, . . .
"O, yes, yes, in there," said Toad *impatiently*.
"Certainly not!" replied Toad *emphatically*.
"Very well, then," said the Badger *firmly* . . . .

*Exercise* 1
What words could you use with *replied* or *said* to suggest a state of sorrow, joy, surprise, delight? Avoid making up adverbs for these words, like sorrowfully. Find another word or phrase.

## F

Here is a poem by Coleridge. It isn't his best poem, but it does explain what is so often done with words today. He speaks of using abstract words to cover up real situations or feelings. Another term for this is *euphemism*. All one has to do is to look at newspaper reports to find examples. *Safeguard* isn't a deodorant; it's a missile system. It may or may not protect, but it sounds as if it would because safe and guard have that connotation. *Pacification* instead of meaning appeasement often meant destroying villages to find the Viet Cong—a bloody, destructive process. *Pacification* sounds better.

*Abstraction*[7]

BOYS AND GIRLS
And women, that would groan to see a child
Pull off an insect's leg, all read of war,
The best amusements for our morning meal!
The poor wretch who has learned his only prayers
From curses, who knows scarcely words enough
To ask a blessing from his Heavenly Father,
Becomes a fluent phraseman, absolute
And technical in victories and defeats,
And all our dainty terms for fratricide;
Terms which we trundle smoothly o'er our tongues

[7] Huxley, Aldons, Ed., *Texts and Pretexts* (New York: Harper & Bros., 1933), p. 169.

> Like mere abstractions, empty sounds to which
> We join no meaning and attach no form
> As if the soldier died without a wound:
> As if the fibres of this godlike frame
> Were gored without a pang: as if the wretch
> Who fell in battle, doing bloody deeds,
> Passed off to Heaven translated and not killed;
> As though he had no wife to pine for him,
> No God to judge him.

This use of words to cover up is not only a product of this poet's day. It is even more true, it seems, in our own.

*Exercise* 1

Find five euphemisms, cover-up words, in newspaper accounts or five you hear on TV broadcasts.

## G

Finally, of course, there are the words which are appropriate or inappropriate, fitting or unfitting. Some writers, hoping for a quick profit, deal in sensationalism, choosing taboo words, those considered unacceptable, to shock their readers. (And people do seem to look for the shocking book or the shocking passages.) In a society as complex as ours, this problem of taboo words is also more complex than it was in a smaller society. What is taboo in one group may not be in another. But I sometimes wonder if the writer isn't sometimes lazy. He need not always substitute a mild "gee-whiz" for a good "God-damn," but neither exclamation really explains the situation. I can vent my feelings in an exclamation, but this doesn't tell the reader the extent of my feeling.

Erasmus, a scholar of a much earlier day (the one who wrote texts for the English school, St. Paul's), put words into groups. His classifications are still, it seems to me at least, quite helpful for writers.

*Exercise* 1

Here are the classifications of Erasmus.[8] Can you think of words which could go into some, if not all, of these groups?

---

[8] Desiderius Erasmus of Rotterdam, *On Copia of Words and Ideas,* translated by Donald B. King and H. David Rix (Milwaukee, Wisc.: Marquette University Press, 1963), pp. 20–23.

1. *Low words.* These do not live up to the dignity of the subject. There is often an avoidance of earthy words. Gardeners buy "fertilizer" not manure. In books about China, the gathering of "night soil" is the translation of the term used for human excrement.

2. *Unusual words.*

> "Horace [the Roman satirist] remarks:
> "Many words will be born again that now are
>   dead,
> And many will die that now are honored—if
>   usage wills.'"

In his day Erasmus felt that writers often used big or unusual words for effect. He felt we should remember that people created language, that it is always changing. Use language people will understand.

3. *Poetic words.* A poet may say "eve" instead of evening, "o'er" for over. In prose, Erasmus noted, use such words sparingly.

4. *Archaic words.* These can be effective. They are more often found in writing which tries to reproduce a historical period.

5. *Obsolete words.* Words which are no longer used.

6. *Harsh words.* Erasmus said Horace objected to the writer who said: "Jupiter spit snow all over the wintry Alps." (Jupiter was king of the gods so spitting sounds undignified.)

7. *New Words.* Writers do coin words. The slang that becomes established creates new words for the language.

8. *Foreign words.* Used because they fit the occasion or the character these can be acceptable. *Senor* would be all right in a story of Mexico or California, out-of-place in Massachusetts. Never use foreign words just to show off.

9. *Obscene words.* Erasmus felt that the usage of the culture determines these. He states, "Words that are manifestly obscene should be completely avoided. Those that are indifferent can be applied in a decent sense." Probably it all goes back to the writer's sense of his readers. (Classification of obscenity seems to belong to every age. What do you think about it?)

*Exercise 2*

About words, Freya Stark[9] says:

Every country has its own way of saying things. The important point is that which lies *behind* people's words, and the art of discovering what this is may be

---

[9] Freya Stark, *Baghdad Sketches* (New York: E. P. Dutton and Co., Inc., 1938), p. 85.

considered as a further step in the learning of languages, of which grammar and syntax are only the beginning. But if we listen to words merely, and give them our own habitual values, we are bound to go astray.

Take a word like *communism*. Would you, as a Russian, have the same feeling about it as the American has?

Find a word which you use that could have a different meaning for others.

CHAPTER THREE

# THE SENTENCE: A FLEXIBLE STRUCTURE

In judo it is important to throw your opponent by making use of his loss of balance. The beginner, therefore, tries to retain his balance or to move so quickly that his opponent may not perceive or take advantage of any momentary loss as he shifts to another hold.

Yet in writing we are singularly incompetent or incapable in this respect. Many a student writer is off-balance much of the time, producing muddy prose which allows the reader to throw the writer, not done physically but in terms of "I don't agree," "He's stupid," "It doesn't say anything."

If the student writer only realized it, his reader is off-balance much of the time. His ideas may be hazy; his experiences felt but not really recognized. He is ready to be "thrown" or persuaded by the writer. Good sentences, like words, allow the writer to do this.

First forget all those stuffy definitions of a sentence as a subject and predicate or as a complete thought, and the stern direction never to use a fragment or (heaven help us) a run-on sentence. Concentrate instead upon the idea that as a child you learned to use sentences and that, as an individual who speaks, you have been using sentences for years.

It is true, however, that the sentences of conversation are not quite like the ones we write. You can call one another damned fools orally but smile in such a way that the listener knows you simply mean that he has done something slightly silly. Or people talk in fragments, completing another's idea. The battery in the car is dead and the answer to the question "What will you do?" might be a complete sentence "I'll call the garage" or perhaps a one word answer "Walk." The waitress asks a complete question: "What will you have?" The customer says "Coffee." Daily conversation is filled with fragments. So, too, is written conversation likely to be, for here the author tries to reproduce the oral language in writing. But if a fragment will befuddle the reader, drop the fragment for a more complete structure.

No one can possibly, however, indicate in writing all the gestures and intonations which go along with oral conversation. The exclamation point will not produce the sensation of horror, though students sometimes seem to think this is true. Writing "It was funny!" or "I was horrified!" neither amuses nor terrifies the reader.

Nor will any one sentence tell us all. Many a man, expressing wishes for his personal future, may say "I have a dream." But when Martin Luther King, Jr. followed "I have a dream" with his desires for his people, it became a goal.

## A

Sentences are important. In the English language the basic sentence patterns are really quite simple:

Birds fly.
Planes fly high.
The meat is tough.
She is here.
The boy is my brother.
He drove the car.
Give the box to me.
We thought the movie exciting.
The boys elected John captain.

But all of us make additions, rearrange the patterns. This chapter, therefore, will deal with the ways to vary our sentences; for it is, really, a compiling of effective sentences in a logical, organized order that creates a persuasive appeal or throws the opponent.

To learn to do this takes practice, and you won't get nearly as many bumps as the judo player does in learning to fall. After all, he is learning a new art while you have the essence of yours, for you already use sentences.

*Exercise* 1

One way to change sentences is, of course, to vary the words. Erasmus, who lived long ago, worked out this exercise. He used a basic sentence:

Your letter delighted me very much.

Erasmus made over 200 changes, some very elaborate.

*a.* "What wine is to a man thirsting for it, your letter is to me."

*b.* "Do not believe that Fortune can offer anything more pleasing than your letter."

*c.* Or, more simply, he wrote "Your letter brought me greater joy than I can express."

Create ten variations of your own on this sentence.

*Note:* If you have difficulty with this, divide into groups and work together.

(1) Choose a committee from the class to go over the individual sentences and make a list of the best ones to read to the class.

## B

In the following exercises you are asked to retell a story, but each exercise calls for a different kind of sentence structure. In a whole composition, all kinds are used, but it is better to practice one kind at a time. This step-by-step method may seem dull, but it is the way you learned to walk. It is odd in a way that we have borrowed from the Greeks their idea of practice for competitive sports, yet so often have neglected their idea of practice for any kind of mental activity.

The first kind is the simple sentence:

Androcles was a soldier.
He shot better than the king.
This made the king his enemy.

But such baby sentences are dull, so you can add:

Extra word and phrase
Androcles, *a favorite of the king,* shot
extra word                          extra phrase
the *king's* deer. The king, *annoyed by this,*
extra phrase
sold Androcles *as a slave.*

These are still simple sentences, but they are not so dull.

The one kind of sentence you must *not* use is the one with a sentence inside the other:

Extra sentence
Androcles *who had been the king's favorite*
extra sentence
shot the deer *that the king had missed.*

30   RHETORICAL TACTICS

*Exercise* 1

Read the following story. Then retell it in declarative (simple) sentences. Extra words and phrases can be used. See if you can't create an interesting story with just the simple sentence and, probably, extra words and phrases.

### *Androcles and the Lion*[1]

Androcles was a brave soldier and one of the emperor's favorites. But once he displeased the emperor by shooting a deer or a boar that the emperor had missed. So the man was sold to be a slave and sent far from his home.

After being a slave for some time, Androcles managed to escape, and wandered off in the hills and deserts, trying to find his way back to his own land. One very hot day he crawled into a cave to get out of the sun. He was very hungry, but hoped he could find something to eat later in the day. While he was resting from his wanderings, he heard a strange sound. He knew that an animal was coming into the cave. But he could not tell what it was. The steps did not sound like the steps of any animal that he knew. But he was frightened, and he held his breath so as to make no sound by which the animal could find him.

As he waited there, holding his breath, the animal came nearer. It was a lion. But he did not look fierce. He did not walk as if he were the King of Beasts. In fact, he was limping on three legs, holding one of his front paws in the air. He looked very unhappy indeed for a lion.

Androcles felt so sorry for the lion that he forgot to be afraid. The lion walked up to him and stopped right there in front of him. He held up his paw and made a soft miaow, like a sad and hungry kitten, only louder. Then Androcles saw that the poor lion had a thorn in his paw. That was why the lion was so mild and so unhappy. He could not put his foot down as firmly as a lion should.

Androcles bent over and gently pulled the thorn out of the lion's foot. It must have hurt, for the lion squeaked a little. But it probably did not hurt as much as walking on the thorn did. The lion purred and shook his head gently at Androcles, then turned around and walked out of the cave.

Androcles wandered about for days and weeks, living as best he could on roots and berries and nuts. At last he came to a camp made up of many tents. He was very glad, because he thought that now he could get food and be

---

[1] Sidonie Matsoner Gruenberg, comp., *Favorite Stories Old and New* (Revised and enlarged ed.; Garden City, N.Y.: Doubleday & Company, 1955), pp. 414–17.

safe from wild animals. But when he came to the camp he saw that it was filled with the emperor's soldiers and the captain recognized Androcles. They made a prisoner of him and after a while brought him back to Rome.

The emperor disliked Androcles even more now, because he had run away from his master. So the emperor decided on a very cruel punishment. He ordered Androcles put into the arena, where a hungry lion should destroy him. There Androcles was, and the gate to the lion's cage was opened.

The lion came out growling and sniffing. He walked about as if he were looking for something to eat. Pretty soon he came to where Androcles was lying on the ground, expecting to be devoured the very next minute. But when the lion stood over Androcles, instead of springing on him he began to lick him gently with his tongue.

Everybody was amazed, and they soon brought word to the emperor that Androcles must be a strange magician, for the lion would not eat him, as lions had always eaten other prisoners. The emperor ordered Androcles brought before him and asked him to explain what his power was that protected him from the lion.

Then Androcles told the story of the lion in the desert, from whose foot he had removed the thorn. The emperor forgave him and took him back into his favor.

*Exercise 2*

This time summarize the story in indirect discourse. This calls for a sentence within a sentence, one almost always introduced by *that* or occasionally by *what*. Variation in the rather gossipy introductory part of the sentence is needed to keep this summary from becoming dull, as in the following examples:

We hear that Androcles shot the king's deer.
It is reported that ——
The story runs that ——
History says that——

*Exercise 3*

Here is the interrogative method of telling the tale. It doesn't matter what kind of structure the sentence has so long as it asks a question. This was, according to the Greeks, the cross-questioning of the trial, still used today. Thus it starts:

Was not Androcles a king's favorite until he shot the king's deer?
Write the summary with this kind of sentence.

*Note:* This kind of sentence can occasionally be most effective in persuasive writing, as it allows the author to give his own answer, one he wants his reader to accept.

*Exercise* 4

The Greeks called this next form the enumerative method. Here you give a number of the ideas in one sentence.

>Androcles, the friend of the king, killed the king's deer, angered the king, was made a slave.

Write your summary using this method, the story should be much shorter.

## C

A good exercise to test your ability to read and to write is to put another's ideas into your own words.

*Exercise* 1

Read this short poem by Carl Sandburg. Although it begins, quite simply, by telling what a fence keeps out, the last line says it is not a complete barrier. In your own words tell in a sentence what he is really saying.

### A Fence[2]

Now the stone house on the lake front is finished
    and the workmen are beginning the fence.
The palings are made of iron bars with steel
    joints that can stab the life out of any
    man who falls on them.
As a fence, it is a masterpiece, and will shut
    off the rabble and all vagabonds and hungry
    men and all wandering children looking for
    a place to play.
Passing through the bars and over the steel
    points will go nothing except Death and
    the Rain and Tomorrow.

*Exercise* 2

Servan Shreiber[3] in his book *The Spirit of May* tells of a demonstration at

---

[2] Carl Sandburg, *The American Tradition in Literature,* revised, edited by Sculley Bradley, Richmond Beatty, and E. Hudson Long (New York: W. W. Norton & Company, Inc., 1961), p. 1300.

[3] J. J. Servan Shreiber, *The Spirit of May* (New York: McGraw-Hill Book Co., 1969), p. 74.

the Tomb of the Unknown Soldier in Paris. Many felt that the students' attitude was highly disrespectful. Here is his comment. In your own words, what is he saying?

In the name of life and freedom the students called a halt to absolute respect for death by command. This was perhaps the first serious homage ever rendered to the Unknown Soldier.

*Exercise 3*

Supposedly there was a writer of long ago named Longinus[4] who gave some ideas for writing sentences. What does he say in the following paragraph? Notice that he defines the word "prolixity" for you.

*Note:* This matter of giving a word and then following it with a definition of its meaning is a common procedure. Unfortunately, when our textbooks called this "a noun in apposition," it was often just confusing.

Another factor which diminishes greatness [He means great writing.] is excessively concise language, for grandeur is maimed when forced into too small a mold. I do not mean unnecessary compactness but a continuous succession of small bits of sentences. Such shortened clauses break the sequence of thought, whereas brevity goes straight to the point. On the other hand, prolixity, length which the occasion does not require, is clearly deadening.

*Exercise 4*

Another way to help us with sentences is to look at those others wrote. The following are two passages describing a storm at sea. The author who quotes these two passages prefers the second one. In your own words can you tell why you think he made this choice?

   *a.* It is a marvel to us, to our minds,
      That men should dwell at sea, so far from land.
      Unfortunate creatures, many ills are theirs,
      Their eyes fixed on the sky, their minds on the deep.
      Often to heaven they raise up their hands
      In a sad prayer from their heaving hearts.
   *b.* He rushed upon them, as a wave storm-driven,
      Boisterous beneath black clouds, on a swift ship
      Will burst, and all is hidden in the foam;
      Meanwhile the wind tears thundering at the mast,

---

[4] Dionysius Cassius Longinus, *On Great Writing* (New York: The Bobbs-Merrill Company, Inc., Liberal Arts Press, 1957), p. 54.

And all hands tremble, pale and sore afraid,
As they are carried close from under death.
[Not the ship, but the wave will burst.
"Boisterous beneath black clouds" describes the wave.][5]

*Exercise 5*

If Eldridge Cleaver stuck to just one sentence structure of noun, verb, noun, plus a couple of phrases like:

"You hear a lot of jazz about Soul Food."[6]

his writing might become dull to the reader. So writers add to the basic sentence or change it around. See how Langston Hughes has reversed the ordinary pattern.

*Afro-American Fragment*[7]

So long,
So far away
Is Africa.

a. Turn this into the ordinary prose sentence.
b. Try composing a sentence like this, using the author's form.

# D

At times, however, the repetition of a basic form can be very effective. In order to keep the close relationship of this series of thoughts, notice that the author connected them by semicolons, rather than using a period and treating each unit as a separate sentence.

*Note:* Punctuation is merely a visual way of representing the intonation or pauses made in speaking. Commas are short pauses. Periods and semicolons are longer ones.

The first thing they had to realize was that all of them were brothers; oppression made them brothers; exploitation made them brothers; degradation made them brothers; discrimination made them brothers; humiliation made them brothers.[8]

---

[5] Dionysius Cassius Longinus, *On Great Writing* (New York: Bobbs-Merrill Library of Liberal Arts, 1957), p. 18. Grubbs, G. M. A., translator.

[6] Eldridge Cleaver, *Soul on Ice* (New York: Dell Publishing Co., 1968), p. 29.

[7] Abraham Chapmen, ed., *Black Voices* (New York: New American Library, 1968), p. 429.

[8] Malcolm X, *Malcolm X Speaks* (New York: Grove Press, 1965), p. 67.

*Exercise 1*

Try writing a similar sentence in which each unit is in the form of the first and all are related.

*Exercise 2*

The following paragraph from *The New Yorker* of May 16, 1970,[9] sums up what was the result of the war in Vietnam, and, at that date, its extension into Cambodia. Each sentence has a basic noun, verb, noun structure. This could grow tiresome. Here its repetition serves to emphasize an idea, each sentence pounding home the thought.

The war has deepened every social and racial and economic division in our society. The war has destroyed our confidence in ourselves as a people and in many of the traditions and freedoms by which we once identified ourselves. The war has made us warlike. The war has so dulled our moral capacities as to make some of our soldiers capable of mass murder and some of our civilians capable of applauding or willfully ignoring that murder. The war has caused us to be scorned or feared or detested by other nations. The war, in its infinite prolongation, has made impossible any realistic consideration of the immediate crises in ecology, in race, in urban decay, in poverty, in education, and in the daily content of life which now await us. The war, in its recent extension and in the manner of that extension, has deepened all these divisions and crises, and has made us suspicious of our leaders and cynical about their ability to lead us and their willingness to hear us. The war must be ended. The war must be ended now.

Try such a paragraph on your own, perhaps shorter. You could use a verb of present time as well.

*Examples:* Schools do (or do not) ─────.
Our environment is ─────.
I believe that ─────.
My community needs ─────.

## E

Varying the usual order of a sentence can be effective as seen in Exercise C-5. Here Jean Toomer[10] does it. Notice the first three sentences especially.

Up from the skeleton stone walls, up from the rotting floor boards the solid

---

[9] *The New Yorker,* May 16, 1970, p. 35.
[10] Jean Toomer, *Cane* (New York: Harper & Row, 1969), p. 51.

hand-hewn beams of oak of the pre-war cotton factory, dusk came. Up from the dusk the full moon came. Glowing like a fired pine-knot, it illumined the great door and soft showered the Negro shanties aligned along the single street of factory town. The full moon in the great door was an omen. Negro women improvised songs against its spell.

Try to imitate one of the sentences from the above paragraph.

# F

But authors not only change patterns, they add to them. Here the simple sentence:

"Once before two images of America came into conflict."

becomes a much longer and more informational one by the addition of a phrase and a clause.

*Note:* The commas set off these additions, since the intonation of our language demands that we pause slightly as we come to additions.

Once before, during the bitter struggle between North and South climaxed by the Civil War, the two images of America came into conflict, although whites North and South scarcely understood it.[11]

*Exercise 1*

Write a sentence in which you use an *although* clause, either at the beginning or the end of the sentence.

*Exercise 2*

You have sometimes been cautioned about using too many compound sentences, simple sentences joined by *and*. In this case, however, when Edmund Burke[12] is urging Parliament to use conciliation rather than force with the American colonies, since force is temporary and uncertain, his "and" sentence is most effective because of the balanced structure and the contrasting ideas concerning the use of force.

> Terror is not always the effect of force, and
> an armament is not a victory.

Try writing a sentence of this kind. Notice the balanced quality, almost like balancing a scale.

---

[11] Eldridge Cleaver, *Soul on Ice* (New York: Dell Publishing Co., 1968), p. 75.

[12] Edmund Burke, *Speech on Conciliation with the Colonies* (Gateway ed.; Chicago: Henry Regnery Co., 1964), p. 60.

*Exercise 3*

Here is a paragraph from a speech made by Black Hawk to General Street after Black Hawk's defeat and capture in 1832.[13] This time, instead of imitating the style of the sentences (although you might try this if you wish), tell what you notice about the sentences.

> I saw my evil day at hand. The sun rose dim on us in the morning, and at night it sank in a dark cloud, and looked like a ball of fire. That was the last sun that shone on Black Hawk. His heart is dead, and no longer beats quick in his bosom. He is now a prisoner of the white men; they will do with him as they wish. But he can stand torture, and is not afraid of death. He is no coward. Black Hawk is an Indian. He has done nothing for which an Indian ought to be ashamed. He has fought for his countrymen, against white men, who came, year after year, to cheat them and take away their lands.

# G

Here is a paragraph of explanation. Although it, too, contains phrases and clauses, expanding the basic sentence, notice that none are there to add color to the paragraph and that all the sentences follow the normal word order of our language.

Judo is a derivative of jujitsu and is the correct term used to refer to the sport form of that art in today's language. The word judo specifically explains the truer meaning of the art as it is practiced today. The *ju* part of the word means "gentleness" or "giving way" and implies a flexibility of techniques, while the *do* part means "way" and signifies the application of the *ju* principle in the execution of the techniques, not only in the physical exertions of the judoka but also in his mental attitude. The older *jitsu* which was replaced by *do,* meant "technique" or "art."[14]

*Exercise 1*

Explain to someone, perhaps an exchange student from another country, what is meant by a term used by students in your school.

# H

Judo could still keep the techniques of the martial art of jujitsu, but modern composition can hardly follow all the ancient rhetorical

---

[13] William Jennings Bryan, ed., *The World's Famous Orations,* Vol. VIII (New York: Funk & Wagnalls Company, 1906), p. 23.

[14] Jiichi Watanabe and Lindy Avakian, *The Secrets of Judo* (Tokyo, Japan and Rutland, Vermont: Charles E. Tuttle Company, 1960), p. 17.

rules for sentences. For Greek and Latin are not English. Ours is a language of word order. *John threw the ball* makes sense. *The ball threw John* doesn't. The periodic sentence of the Latin writer, one where the main idea comes at the end of the sentence, seems awkward when we usually begin with the main idea.

As long as Latin was the language of scholars and of writers this did not matter; the trouble came when the composition texts quoted the Latin rules for English.

Frequently the modern writer starts with a simple sentence, but instead of using a period and beginning a new sentence, he adds to the old one material which expands and adds to the statement. To do this means observing more closely than many people do. They say "It's a hot day." But how hot is it? Is the asphalt melting? Is the sun burning? Is everyone wiping away the sweat? These are the details that count.

The late Professor Christensen observed, after study of much modern writing, that authors use a simple sentence and then add. Such additions lend vitality to an author's style. As a beginning teacher I knew one paper was better than another but could only say it sounded better and was not sure how to explain why. Now I realize that a sentence or so of this kind probably created this impression. This is a sentence technique of professional writers, used particularly in narration and description. It is easily learned and practical and it does improve writing. Here are five simple sentences:

1. A feeble light burned above the entrance.
2. I handed it over.
3. She knelt by him.
4. Bond walked warily through the trees.
5. Little sunshine could enter their world.

Now notice how much more you learn when a detail is added.

1. "A feeble light burned above the entrance, sparkling the snow."
—Ralph Ellison[15]

2. "I handed it over, noticing the gold links in the soft white cuffs as he extended his hand." —Ralph Ellison[16]

[15] Ralph Ellison, *The Invisible Man* (New York: New American Library, 1968), p. 292.
[16] *Ibid.*, p. 159.

3. "She knelt by him, sobbing."        —Madeleine L'Engle[17]
4. "Bond walked warily through the trees, watching each step for dead branches."        —Ian Fleming[18]
5. "Little sunshine could enter their dim world, penetrating the cloud banks from which fell the endless rains."        —Rachel Carson[19]

Now it would be possible to put this addition, "sparkling the snow," at the beginning or in the middle of the sentence.

>Sparkling the snow, a feeble light burned
>above the entrance.
>A feeble light, sparkling the snow, burned
>above the entrance.

Sometimes these additions are short, sometimes long. They usually start with an *-ing* form of the verb.

In this sentence, you can see how Eldridge Cleaver[20] has used several of these additions to describe the effect of Elvis Presley's songs, certainly more effective than the basic sentence: So Elvis Presley came.

So Elvis Presley came, strumming a weird guitar and wagging his tail across the continent, ripping off fame and fortune as he scrunched his way, and, like a latter day Johnny Appleseed, sowing seeds of a new rhythm and style in the white souls of the white youth of America, whose inner hunger and need was no longer satisfied with the antiseptic white shoes and whiter songs of Pat Boone. "You can do anything," sang Elvis to Pat Boone's white shoes, "but don't you step on my Blue Suede Shoes!"

*Exercise 1*

Try creating this kind of sentence. If everyone takes a basic sentence, such as "I looked at the street," adding details, it is surprising how many different pictures one can get of a street.

*Exercise 2*

A second kind of addition is very simple, putting the adjectives after the noun, not the normal order, or at the end of the sentence. This can be effective.

---

[17] Madeleine L'Engle, *A Wrinkle in Time* (Ariel Books; New York: Farrar, Straus and Giroux, 1962), p. 16.
[18] Ian Fleming, *Goldfinger* (Signet; New York: New American Library, 1959), p. 113.
[19] Rachel Carson, *The Sea Around Us* (New York: New American Library, 1963), p. 23.
[20] Eldridge Cleaver, *Soul on Ice* (New York: Dell Publishing Co., 1968), p. 194.

## 40  RHETORICAL TACTICS

Rachel Carson's[21] "The reptiles for a time dominated the earth, *gigantic, grotesque, terrifying*." seems to say more than if she had placed the terms before the word reptile.

Toomer[22] writes: "Her eyes, if it were sunset, rested idly where the sun, *molten and glorious*, was pouring down between the fringe of pines." This is much better than the usual "She watched the sunset."

From *A Wrinkle in Time*[23] comes this sentence: "The column rose up in the middle of the room, *crystal clear and empty*." The adjectives clarify the meaning of "column."

Write five sentences where you use adjectives as added details. Try to find adjectives which really expand the idea.

*Exercise* 3

Two other kinds of addition may not be found so frequently. One is an addition for explanation, almost a list, usually preceded by a colon.

Thus for one lone stretch of time I lived with the intensity displayed by those chronic numbers players who see clues to their fortune in the most minute and insignificant phenomena: in clouds, on passing trucks and subway cars, in dreams, comic strips, the shape of dog-luck fouled on pavements.[24]

Here is another, details added for explanation in judo.

The stability of any standing object is determined by three factors: weight, base, and position of center of gravity.[25]

*a.* Try writing a sentence which has this kind of listing. An easy one for the housewife might be about shopping in the supermarket. You may prefer: "I watched the crowd: ―――――."

I looked at the vegetables: the brown potatoes, white and yellow onions, green heads of lettuce, carrots, and purple eggplants.

Lists are really easy if you look at situations.

This next addition usually comes directly after some term which it explains. As a scientific writer Rachel Carson[26] often adds definitions in this way:

---

[21] Rachel Carson, *The Sea Around Us* (New York: New American Library, 1963), p. 28.
[22] Jean Toomer, *Cane* (New York: Harper & Row, 1969), p. 51.
[23] Madeleine L'Engle, *A Wrinkle in Time* (Ariel Books; New York: Farrar, Straus and Giroux, 1962), p. 153.
[24] Ralph Ellison, *The Invisible Man* (New York: New American Library, 1968), p. 331.
[25] Jiichi Watanabe and Lindy Avakian, *The Secrets of Judo* (Tokyo, Japan and Rutland, Vermont: Charles E. Tuttle Company, 1960), p. 37.
[26] Rachel Carson, *The Sea Around Us* (New York: New American Library, 1963), p. 42.

## The Sentence: A Flexible Structure 41

Diatoms must have silica, *the element of which their fragile cells are fashioned.*

The simplest form of this addition is the sentence found on the sports pages:

Sikes, a *slim dark Arkansan,* had a final 67.
Carlos, *the San Jose State speedster,* said he will compete in the 1970 indoor season.

*b.* Write a sentence using a word or name which may not be clear to the reader, following it with the explanatory word or phrase.

*Exercise* 4

Occasionally an addition may be almost like a separate sentence. The addition starts with a noun, but could have the preposition *with* before it. In certain cases, it seems more effective without that preposition. Ralph Ellison[27] writes: "The clock, its alarm lost in the larger sound, said seven-thirty, and I got out of bed." Madeleine L'Engle[28] writes: "She walked slowly down the hill, her heart thumping against her ribs."

We might say: It was an old car, its fenders dented, its windshield cracked, its tires worn

Now add details for a new car: It was a new car, its ———, its ———, its ———.

Try this sentence: I saw myself in the mirror, my hair ———, my face ———, etc., etc. Think of your appearance in the morning and write a sentence for that time. Then do one sentence describing what the mirror reflects when you are ready for a party. (If you hesitate to describe yourself, say "The boy," or "The girl," or "The man," or "The woman" saw ———.)

*Exercise* 5

All of the sentences in the preceding four exercises can be called, as Professor Christensen called them, multi-level sentences. The first sentence is the basic one, giving the general idea. The rest makes this thought more specific, expanding or contracting the idea. There may be more than two levels as the element used to describe the basic sentence is itself described in a further word, phrase, or clause.

Here is an example, first written as the regular sentence and then in levels.

---

[27] Ralph Ellison, *The Invisible Man* (New York: New American Library, 1968), p. 276.
[28] Madeleine L'Engle, *A Wrinkle in Time* (Ariel Books; New York: Farrar, Straus, and Giroux, 1962), p. 203.

He played the guitar expertly, moving his hand agilely up and down the neck, each movement throwing drops of perspiration onto his instrument, pressing the strings almost effortlessly and feeling the rhythm of the song.—Student sentence

1 He played the guitar expertly,
    2 moving his hand agilely up and down the neck,
        3 each movement throwing drops of perspiration onto his instrument,
        3 pressing the strings almost effortlessly and feeling the rhythm of the song.

The comma is the clue to the levels, for if the sentence is read aloud there is a pause before the new element begins. The second level, if you notice, describes the basic sentence; the next two elements or number 3 levels tell more of the movement of the hands. The combination of all the levels makes the general statement about playing a guitar much more specific. Some authors use more than two or three levels, and you may want to try this, but first try for two, then three levels. Take the following as a basic sentence or try one of your own:

*a.* The night slowly descended upon the city,
*b.* I was not pleased with the place where I would soon be working,
*c.* Garbage filled the alley,
*d.* The commercial appeared on the TV screen,
*e.* The cars raced down the street,

*Exercise 6*

The Japanese have a three-line poem, the haiku, that is fun to do and gives practice in writing.

There are three lines, five syllables in the first and last line, seven syllables in the second. Each line usually ends in a strong word. There is a reference to time, usually the season. There is likely to be a comparison and the author's feeling is suggested.

If you haven't paid much attention to the rhythm of language, try doing this before writing your haiku. It will help you to get the right number of syllables. Sound out some names: Jerry, Susan. In each case the first part of the name is stressed *Jer* and *Su*. The second part, or second syllable, is said with less force. The name *John* is all one stressed syllable. In your haiku you may find that your stressed and unstressed syllables fall into a kind of pattern. Here are examples:[29]

[29] *Haiku,* translated by Peter Beilenson (Mt. Vernon, N.Y.: Peter Pauper Press, 1956), pp. 8, 39.

## The Sentence: A Flexible Structure 43

> Dead my old fine hopes
> And dry my dreaming, but still . . .
> Iris, blue each spring.   —Shushiki
>
> Angry I strode home . . .
> But stooping in my garden
> Calm old willow-tree.   —Ryota
>
> Trees stand like great kings
> Looking over all mankind,
> Protecting their realm.   —Don Anderson
>
> Snow is like a whip,
> Lashing and stinging your face
> Till cold winds abate.   —Steve Perez

Try writing a haiku of your own.

*Exercise 7*

Find a picture that you feel portrays a definite situation or scene. Exchange pictures and try to write a descriptive sentence about your picture, one that would give the reader the feeling of the picture itself.

# I

Barbara Tuchman[30] writes history, but unlike the authors of your usual textbooks she believes in adding details which give the reader the atmosphere of the time. Thus her book *The Guns of August* covers only the first month of World War I. Read the following excerpts and discuss whether or not these added details give you a better sense of history.

So gorgeous was the spectacle on the May morning of 1910 when nine kings rode in the funeral of Edward VII of England that the crowd, waiting in hushed and black-clad awe, could not keep back gasps of admiration. In scarlet and blue and green and purple, three by three the sovereigns rode through the palace gates, with plumed helmets, gold braid, crimson sashes, and jeweled orders flashing in the sun. After them came five heirs apparent, forty more imperial or royal highnesses, seven queens—four dowager and three regnant—and a scattering of special ambassadors from un-

---

[30] Barbara W. Tuchman, *The Guns of August* (New York: The Macmillan Company, 1962), pp. 1, 185.

crowned countries. Together they represented seventy nations in the greatest assemblage of royalty and rank ever gathered in one place and, of its kind, the last. The muffled tongue of Big Ben tolled nine by the clock as the cortege left the palace, but on history's clock it was sunset, and the sun of the old world was setting in a dying blaze of splendor never to be seen again.

. . . . .

The long-desired moment when the French flag would be raised again in Alsace had come. The covering troops, waiting among the thick, rich pines of the Vosges, trembled with readiness. These were the remembered mountains with their lakes and waterfalls and the damp delicious smell of the forests where fragrant ferns grew between the pines. Hilltop pastures, grazed by cattle, alternated with patches of forest. Ahead, the shadowed purple line of the Ballon d'Alsace, highest point in the Vosges, was hidden in mist. Patrols who ventured to the top could see down below the red-roofed villages of the lost territory, the gray church spires, and the tiny, gleaming line of the Moselle where, young and near its source, it was narrow enough to be waded. Squares of white potato blossom alternated with strips of scarlet-runner beans and gray-green-purple rows of cabbages. Haycocks like small fat pyramids dotted the fields as if arranged by a painter. The land was at its peak of fertility. The sun sparkled over all. Never had it looked so much worth fighting for.

*Note:* Unlike ancient civilizations which carved their sentences on stones, making changes difficult, you can easily erase, cross out, and try again. Don't be afraid to revise. Above all, don't be afraid to put your sentences down on paper. Can you possibly imagine anyone becoming an Olympic champion who never practiced because he might make a mistake? Reading also helps, just any reading, for you unconsciously absorb much of the idea of the written language from the printed page.

CHAPTER FOUR

# THE PARAGRAPH: MAKING AN IDEA CLEAR TO THE READER

Indentation is not the sole indicator of a paragraph. Indentation, like punctuation, is simply another visual sign for the reader. Although in some paragraphs a topic sentence is implied rather than stated, in general the topic sentence indicates the paragraph. It determines the direction the paragraph will take and, if you stray away from this established path by adding irrelevant material, you will only confuse your reader. He is also confused if all he gets is a series of topic sentences, stating different directions but never, since they are not explained, really going anywhere.

Neither can the kinds of paragraphs be completely defined. Although there are some definite variations in the way they are developed. The writer of history states in his topic sentence that there were several reasons for the war and then follows this by listing the reasons. The novelist may say it is a hot day and then describe it. In *The Stranger* by Camus, the author could have taken it for granted that the reader knows Algeria, the place where the novel's action occurs, is hot, but he doesn't. Thus when he describes the movement of the funeral procession along the dusty road he adds details of the heat and glare of the sun.

Another writer may list a point, explain it, and then list another. Or, having stated an idea, the author may prove it by an example, one from literature or from life. He can introduce something he feels the reader will not understand and illustrate by comparison with something the reader knows. But always the paragraph must go with the topic sentence.

There can be no set limits on paragraph length. The writer simply expands his topic sentence until the idea should be, hopefully, clear to the reader. Only the journalist divides a paragraph into parts, and this is done because the narrowness of the newspaper column needs frequent breaks to make reading it easier.

## A

This is a simple exercise in expansion, but it calls for observation. Suppose I write: He was angry. The tendency of the beginner then is to tell why. A reader might like to recognize just how angry the individual was. What expression did he have? Did his eyes glare? Did he clench his fists? Was he so angry he sputtered when he talked? Was his body tense? Answer all these questions and you have a paragraph.

*Exercise* 1

Complete the picture for one of these or choose a similar topic for expansion.
  a. The crowd gathered.
  b. We were afraid.
  c. The store was crowded.
  d. It was an old building.
  e. The weather was hot.

## B

Fables frequently are used for proving a statement in an argument. They end in a moral which is the idea of the topic sentence.

*Exercise* 1

Here is one you probably know: *The Hare and the Tortoise*.

The hare challenged the animals to a race, but only the slow tortoise accepted. The hare, confident of his speed, stopped to rest so many times that the tortoise beat him. Slow and steady wins the race.

Try expanding this fable into a longer paragraph. This gives you a chance to try out your practice with sentences. (If you include conversation, you may have more than one paragraph, as we put the remarks of different characters in separate paragraphs.) The topic sentence might be: Speed doesn't always win. Then follow with the expanded fable. Or, if you prefer, expand any other simple fable or story you know.

## C

Another way to develop a paragraph is to state a bare fact and then give the reasons for it. An educator may write: Many students have a reading problem. But why? Weren't they capable? Was the teaching poor? Should another method of teaching reading have been tried? Did the students feel the material wasn't worth reading? Weren't there any extra books for the students to read?

Here is an example. The topic sentence is the bare fact.

*Many older people resent the youth of today.* They dislike their appearance, different from their established modes of dress and of grooming. They dislike their music and their speech. They recall the depression and think today's kids have an easy life. They wanted to attend college but couldn't; many of today's kids do. More than all this they resent the lack of respect young people have for the kind of world many adults have accepted.

If, however, you have only one or two reasons to offer, it may seem too brief. In this case you expand by adding some description or explanation of the reason.

*Exercise 1*

State a fact. Then give the reasons for it. The number of reasons will determine the length of the paragraph. You may find it necessary to analyze the order of your reasons. Should the most important come first or last? Think of this from the point of view of persuading the reader.

*Exercise 2*

Dickens in his *Tale of Two Cities* has a paragraph describing his age in which he speaks of it as "the best of times, the worst of times." Try expanding a topic like one of these:

*a.* Ours is an age of exploration.
*b.* Ours is an age of war.
*c.* Ours is an age of violence.
*d.* Ours is an age of problems.

Here you might find that your choice determines what you say. Reasons alone might be enough for *d.* In *a* you might find that you concentrated upon explaining just one kind, space exploration.

## D

The rhetoric student of early times was asked to use a fable or an example from history to prove his point. This is effective and was a way to teach the stories of fables and the events of history. We can also, however, use an example of an incident in our own lives, particularly if we think the reader has had a similar experience.

This use of our own experience is useful in more than creating a paragraph. If the reader has had the same kind of experience, it arouses his interest and sympathy. If he hasn't, he is educated and his understanding broadened by what we write.

*Exercise* 1

Here are some proverbs one might use as a topic sentence. Complete the paragraph by giving an example: fable, history, or your own experience. Narration, or telling a story, is the way to develop the paragraph in this case.

  *a.* Little strokes fell great oaks.
  *b.* Honesty is the best policy.
  *c.* Diligence is the mother of good luck.
  *d.* Haste makes waste.

# E

These next exercises (1 through 5) might be considered in the language of warfare, strategies.

One of the exercises given by Hermogenes, a Greek teacher, was a model for a specific kind of paragraph. Unlike others, this one consisted of nine steps, which, when completed, did make a good paragraph.

1. The first step was to find a topic sentence. Hermogenes gave his pupils a proverb by another Greek rhetorician, Isocrates. We might say: "Honesty is the best policy."

2. The second step was called the encomium. This meant saying something in praise of the author of the proverb, such as: "Although others have also used his phrase, Cervantes, the famous Spanish author, coined this sentence."

3. Step three was to paraphrase the topic sentence. Paraphrasing is simply stating the idea over again in one's own words. Example: "A man who is fair and just gets along best in this world."

4. In step four, the student was told to give proof direct. If, for example, the proverb were "Honesty is the best policy," the writer could say: "The honest man wins the respect and trust of his fellow men."

5. Step five is by contrast, so the writer could say: "Though dishonesty may bring results, they may not be satisfactory and disclosure of such behavior is always possible." Shakespeare said, "No legacy is so rich as honesty."

6. Step six was an illustration. Example: "As adulteration destroys food, so do lies destroy character."

7. Step seven is an example. Churchill did not fool his people. He said the war would demand "blood, sweat, toil and tears."

8. The eighth step was by authority. If possible, this means quoting someone else who had said much the same thing as the original proverb.

9. The ninth and last step was called the epilogue. Here one exhorted (urged) the reader to believe that honesty really was the best policy.

*Exercise 1*

Following the nine steps suggested does make a good paragraph. It is not an easy exercise but not quite so difficult as it sounds. One of these sayings might be used as a topic sentence. The authors are probably well-enough known for you to find a word of encomium, or praise, for them for Step 2. Try this as a class exercise at first. Then try it on your own.

   *a.* "Good fences make good neighbors."—Robert Frost
   *b.* "The Honey is sweet, but the Bee has a Sting."—Benjamin Franklin
   *c.* "Half a meal in freedom is better than a full meal in bondage."—Aesop
   *d.* "A hero must be brave in deeds as well as in word."—Aesop
   *e.* "Whoever tries for great objects must suffer something."—Plutarch
   *f.* "The cautious seldom err."—Confucius
   *g.* "He who acts with a constant view to his own advantage will be much murmured against."—Confucius

*Exercise 2*

Another way to develop a paragraph in which the writer wishes to explain or define an idea or a proposition is to begin by telling what it is not. In the following paragraph Edmund Burke,[1] who was urging conciliation with the American colonies, defines the kind of peace he desires. (This paragraph should first be discussed for meaning and then for construction.)

The proposition is peace. Not peace through the medium of war; not peace to be hunted through the labyrinth [winding ways] of intricate and endless negotiations; not peace to arise out of universal discord, fomented from principle, in all parts of the empire; not peace to depend on the juridical determination of perplexing questions, or the precise marking of the shadowy boundaries of a complex government. It is simple peace, sought in its natural course and in its ordi-

---

[1] Edmund Burke, *Speech on Conciliation with the Colonies* (Gateway ed.; Chicago: Henry Regnery Co., 1964), p. 42.

nary haunts. It is peace sought in the spirit of peace, and laid in principles purely pacific. . . .

Of course, the language and style of the eighteenth-century writer is more elaborate than ours as a rule.

But try this kind of exercise. Write a paragraph showing what you mean by friendship, loyalty, hate, love, etc. First tell what it is not, then what it is.

*Exercise 3*

An encomium, or paragraph of praise, was, the early teachers of rhetoric felt, helpful in two ways. It made a good beginning for a longer speech, the kind spoken at the death of great men, or, in court, it was valuable in establishing the good character of the individual, proving probably that he was innocent. Hundreds of years have gone by, but we still use the encomium, although, of course, with variations. The topics followed this order: his race, his city, his family. The next was his training, his education, the kind of life he led, his friends and situation in life. Each of these will, naturally, assist in creating the picture of a worthy character.

The Greek schoolboy frequently chose a historical character for his composition. Today we might prefer to take a living person. Try writing such a paragraph of encomium or praise about a person whom you admire.

*Exercise 4*

Following much the same pattern, these earlier students also wrote paragraphs of vituperation, blame or abuse. In this, everything that is said presents the subject in an unfavorable light. If you dislike some character, either past or present, here is an opportunity to express your feeling. Follow the same pattern as for the paragraph of praise, but in this the person is either a disgrace to his race, friends, training, etc. or his race, family, friends, training, etc. are all despicable.

*Exercise 5*

In the encomium, as well as elsewhere, the writer uses comparisons, incidents which help the reader understand and more fully appreciate the thought of the writer.

Julius Caesar was known as a general, but we still have a few of his speeches. In this one[2] he talked of the treatment of conspirators; his ideas,

---

[2] George W. Hibbitt, ed., *The Dolphin Book of Speeches* (Garden City, N.Y.: Doubleday & Co., Inc., 1965), p. 37.

*The Paragraph: Making an Idea Clear to the Reader* 51

evidently were less blood-thirsty than those of many of his audience. Here is one of his comparisons to prove his point.

Within our own memory, too, when the victorious Sylla ordered Damasippus, and others of similar character, who had risen by distressing their country, to be put to death, who did not commend the proceeding? All exclaimed that wicked and factious men, who had troubled the state with their seditious [traitorous] practices, had justly forfeited their lives. Yet this proceeding was the commencement of great bloodshed. For whenever anyone coveted [desired] the mansion or villa, or even the plate [wealth] or apparel of another, he exerted his influence to have him numbered among the proscribed [listed for death]. Thus they, to whom the death of Damasippus had been a subject of joy, were soon after dragged to death themselves; nor was there any cessation [stopping] of slaughter, till Sylla had glutted all partisans with riches [gotten enough wealth for all his friends].

Here is Malcolm X[3] giving a comparison. His paragraph was in answer to a question about the struggle between capitalism and socialism.

It is impossible for capitalism to survive, primarily because the system of capitalism needs some blood to suck. Capitalism used to be like an eagle, but now it's more like a vulture. It used to be strong enough to go and suck anybody's blood whether they were strong or not. But now it has become more cowardly, like the vulture, and it can only suck the blood of the helpless. As the nations of the world free themselves, then capitalism has less victims, less to suck, and it becomes weaker and weaker. It's only a matter of time in my opinion before it will collapse completely.

Either of these paragraphs might go with a speech of condemnation. Caesar refers to a historical precedent; Malcolm X compares capitalism to a natural object, the vulture.

Choose one characteristic or quality given to the character about whom you wrote in Exercise E-3 or Exercise E-4 and expand it by a comparison.

## F

Many writers of all ages have chosen myths or Biblical stories as a means of illustration and comparison. This may mean that the writer can give an idea more briefly.

For example, in the Trojan War, Odysseus, one of the Greek leaders, had the Greeks set sail, as if they had given up the war, leaving behind

---

[3] Malcolm X, *Malcolm X Speaks* (New York: Grove Press, 1965), p. 199.

only a big wooden horse. Rejoicing at victory, the Trojans dragged the horse within the walls of their city of Troy. But that night the Greek warriors, hidden within the horse, stole out and began to fight. Troy lost.

Eldridge Cleaver[4] uses this story in his chapter: "The Black Man's Stake in Vietnam." He writes: "But at home there is a Trojan Horse, a Black Trojan Horse that has become aware of itself and is now struggling to get on its feet. It, too, demands liberation." The reader who knows the story can sense the extra meaning that the mythical reference gives to this statement.

At times a myth really expands a meaning. In his book *The Souls of Black Folk,* W. E. DuBois[5] deplores the materialism of our country by discussing the city of Atlanta, which, "if not named for Atalanta, she ought to have been." He recalls, to the reader who may have forgotten the story, the misfortune which befell Atalanta and her suitor Hippomones, who won the race which rewarded him with the Greek maiden by tossing three golden apples in her path. But the lovers forgot to thank the gods, profaned the temple of love, and were cursed. So, too, DuBois, as he continues, this time for a series of paragraphs, compares the city to the Greek maiden, deploring that the city too has succumbed to the lure of gold and wealth, to the materialism that seems to be, to many, the only kind of reward.

In another chapter in this book DuBois uses the title "Of the Quest of the Golden Fleece" and again, a knowledge of the story adds to an understanding of his chapter.

*Exercise* 1

Try writing a paragraph which uses a myth to help explain your idea. The story of King Midas might be used to discuss greed, Daedalus and Icarus as an example of youth's lack of judgment, or poor Arachne the fault of being too proud.

*Note:* These names may be strange to you and these stories unknown, for readers used in our schools have sometimes neglected them. Originally, of course, these stories served to explain, as when Phaethon let the chariot of the sun god get too near the earth, drying it up and creating the Sahara

---

[4] Eldridge Cleaver, *Soul on Ice* (New York: Dell Publishing Co., 1968), p. 122.

[5] W. E. DuBois, *The Souls of Black Folk* (Greenwich, Conn.: Fawcett Publications, Inc., 1961).

desert. As time went on, myths were used to explain or to point a moral. Thus Phaethon should never have been driving in the first place. He lacked experience. He wanted to show off his relation to Apollo, the sun god.

*Note:* There are inexpensive editions of these stories and they might prove interesting reading. At the very least you will find out why the space agency calls men "astronauts" and names space programs "Apollo."

*Greek Gods and Heroes* by Robert Graves—Dell Publishing Company, New York, 1965.

*Mythology—Timeless Tales of Gods and Heroes* by Edith Hamilton—New American Library (A Mentor book), New York, 1942.

*Men and Gods* by Rex Warner—Avon Publishing Company, New York, 1969.

*Exercise 2*

Biblical stories may be used as a way of expanding a topic sentence. Sermons often consist of a statement followed by a Biblical example. The story of David and Jonathan is frequently used as a reference to a devoted friendship. If a man is trying to do something against great odds, then he is the David going against the mighty Goliath. Try using a Biblical story to expand an idea.

*Note:* The stories referred to can be found in the Bible, the first book of Samuel. Like the myths, the Bible stories can be entertaining as well as useful.

Thus a whole composition will be simply a collection of paragraphs. While each paragraph expands or explains, in one way or another the main idea of the paragraph, all of them together must serve to persuade the reader that the author's subject is one deserving of consideration.

CHAPTER FIVE

# THE PROPOSITION: THE THESIS STATEMENT THE WRITER MUST PROVE

Quite simply, the proposition or thesis statement is the statement of the stand the writer takes on a subject, but finding the subject and determining this thesis is not easy. In theory, if a writer has the facts, he can argue equally well that something should or should not be done, but in practice he does better to choose a subject he knows and a thesis in which he sincerely believes.

The neglect of this aspect of personal interest in a subject and the subsequent thesis statement has added to the difficulties some students already have with writing compositions. Perhaps because of the frequent question: "What can I write about?" teachers responded by relieving their students of this responsibility and assigned subjects for compositions, although this may have been only a title implying a subject. Some of these suggestions, those more closely related to student interests, produced better compositions than the others; but a poor result was more likely to be attributed to a lack of student effort on the assigned topic rather than the subject itself.

Even when teachers permitted students to choose their own subjects, the results were not much better. With only a vague idea of a subject in mind, students turned to reference books and encyclopedias, and while papers composed mainly from such sources were not condemned in the lower grades, they later drew comments about plagiarism. Some students have resurrected past papers for a present assignment; others have asked those with a flair for writing to do the paper. Such practices may have won a grade but did nothing to further the student's ability to write. But moralizing about the ethics of these methods of doing a paper will not cause change. Students must be shown how to find a subject which interests them and a thesis they really want to prove.

Such thesis statements may come from a lively class discussion. I recall that in a junior high class the subject of community improvements called forth so many ideas that I suggested a short paper on the subject. Since many in the class lived in an unpaved area, they chose paving, and I could almost choke on the dust as these pupils described the existing conditions. These papers were better than usual because the writers knew their subject. Yet assignments for writing practice can hardly wait upon chance class discussions. These can, however, be stimulated by reading, if in discussions of the problems related by the author, you and others in the class see their relationship to your own lives. While the books concerned with mankind's problems are not always easy reading, it does seem as if students can read anything which seems to relate to their own lives.

Suppose, for example, you read *Malcolm X*. Here is a man who became a leader. But what made him one? This leads into all kinds of fascinating paths and to other books. Does the leader make himself? Do the people do it? Does he follow the ideas of his age or does he suggest new ideas which the people follow? To the early Greeks, Achilles was a hero because he could kill the greatest warrior in the Trojan forces. But is that our idea of a hero now? What do our leaders substitute for such physical combat? All of this might lead to a composition on what made Malcolm X a leader.

Again you might note if you engaged in a discussion of this book that the reading he did in prison had an effect upon the future life of Malcolm X. Someone might remember that Eldridge Cleaver talked about the reading he did in prison or that Thoreau's essay on *Civil Disobedience* resulted from a jail sentence. This does not imply, of course, that prison is necessary for either reading or study, but it might bring up the subject of how lives are affected by circumstances.

A class reading Conrad's *Heart of Darkness* could consider both the way in which his experiences developed the character of the author and the way in which he used his experiences to develop the fiction. Joseph Conrad's earlier journey through the Belgian Congo enabled him to create Kurtz, a character whose life was ruined because, away from civilization, all he wanted was ivory and ruthlessly exploited the natives to obtain it. Thus one person might choose to write of the way this author presented colonial exploitation, while another would discuss exploitation in his own society. Still others in the class might write of how greed destroys character. In this last instance greed need not be just that of Kurtz, the fictional character, but the destructive force of greed as applied to the man of today.

For even while fiction may seem remote from your life, it can provide clues leading to a subject and a thesis statement you can use for a composition. The very title of one of Chinua Achebe's novels, *Things Fall Apart,* could suggest a subject, for while his characters lived in nineteenth-century Nigeria, things still fall apart, for societies as well as individuals.

Less remote from your daily existence are the articles in newspapers and magazines, the speeches you hear on TV. All of these, if you start to discuss them, yield material for compositions. Notice the way people gather in small groups for a coffee-break. The conversation may be trivial, but an alert member of the group may find even there a proposition he wishes to prove or disprove.

Despite all this, some students will never find satisfactory thesis statements because they feel that writing is not useful. Until they realize that learning to persuade others and learning how to recognize the biased or slanted opinions we get, both orally and in writing, they will regard writing compositions as just another kind of educational drill. Yet people are more confident when they can express themselves clearly. A man has more pride in himself if he can explain how he feels and perhaps be successful in persuading others that his ideas are honest and worthwhile.

## A

Now even after amassing material about your subject, you still need to formulate the thesis statement, the declaration of the idea you wish the reader to accept. At times, as in the class discussion of a piece of writing, the thesis statement may readily come to mind. But this is not always true, for it is possible to be interested in a subject, know quite a bit about it, and yet be uncertain as to how to word your statement. In such circumstances, you might be helped by the three questions used by the rhetorician in the Roman era to determine the point of issue in a court trial. The first asked "Is it a question of fact?" In other words: "Did A really assault B?" The second was a question of definition: "Was it a planned assault, or did A just accidentally knock B into the gutter?" The third was a question of quality or of what kind of assault it was: "Did A act in self-defense or was he actuated by some provocation on B's part?" The story goes that in Cicero's day a Roman soldier was actually acquitted of murdering a general because of the third question. The general, they decided, was such a worthless man he merited being killed.

Here is one example of the use of these questions. Suppose that the students are upset about a rising cost in meals in the school cafeteria. The first question would determine the fact. Have the prices really increased or is this a rumor?

Then comes definition. If the rising cost has been determined as a fact, then is this a cost for the same amount of food or will a sandwich now be included in the price for soup?

Finally, of course, is the question of quality. Is this rise in cost justified? Have rising food prices made it impossible to serve the same amount for the old price?

The answers to these questions should be easy for you to get, for not only did you pay more but you also have the article in the school paper notifying the student body of this change in cost. And when your tray carried the same lunch as before but you paid ten cents more, you know the answer to the second question. It becomes fairly obvious then that your composition will deal with an answer to question three, and you start to formulate your thesis statement. This should be in *one* declarative sentence, so you write: Prices for food are too high. This could mean food prices for the entire country, too extensive a thesis. Or you could narrow it somewhat by stating: Students pay too much for food. This might take in all schools and all students. Stick to your own situation, the one for which you can get definite facts: The new prices for food in our cafeteria are too high for many students. (And even this may mean finding out more facts. The testimony from a few of your friends isn't adequate proof.)

This necessity to limit the scope of the composition, since its length is determined by the breadth of the thesis statement, is admittedly difficult. In class, perhaps, if you had been discussing the Conrad story mentioned earlier, you might have suggested for your thesis statement: Exploitation is evil. Hearing this, the instructor or other students might have asked: What exploitation? How is it evil? How are these defined? Do you mean in connection with the story or in your community? Such comments early in the game can point the way to a more limited thesis statement. But not all subjects will be discussed in class. What you learned from comments there, you must later do on your own.

For instance, a Ralph Nader can write a book *Unsafe at Any Speed,* pointing out flaws in the production of cars. You might write one proving that in your case the warranty did not live up to its claims. A John Holt may write a book on *How Children Fail;* you can write on the ineffective way you were taught reading or arithmetic. (Notice I said reading *or* arithmetic. You can't do justice to two subjects in one composition.) A college student writes: College administration is too complex. What he really wants to prove is the narrower topic: There should be a more effective method for dropping and adding courses.

*Exercise* 1

Here are some topics upon which you may have ideas. Work out thesis statements for three of them, remembering that each statement must be a declarative sentence and that it must not cover more than you can prove in a page or two of writing.

| | |
|---|---|
| The professional athlete | Our courts |
| Individual film-making | Status symbols |
| Employment practices | Cost of living |
| Communication media | Entertainment groups |
| New theories of education | Paperback favorites |

Undoubtedly, as a first attempt, your statement will be too broad. Discuss the various statements in class, trying to narrow each one, or at least several, to manageable size.

*Exercise* 2

Here are some thesis statements written by students who had been reading an article concerned with education.

*a.* A college degree does not qualify a person for a job.

*b.* American education is too materialistically oriented; Americans concern themselves with making money and neglect art, literature, philosophy, and science.

*c.* Today's education should be directed toward analysis and reasoning and away from merely stuffing useless information into students.

*d.* A liberal education is essential to the maturity of a man or woman.

*e.* The American educational system has undergone a vast change in the past fifty years.

Let's consider these thesis statements. The one in *a* does not tell the kind of degree or the kind of job. There are many jobs for which a college degree is not necessary, yet probably most of us would assume that a college degree would not bar one from many kinds of work. We also realize that a college degree does not automatically create the kind of character an employer may desire. Or might this mean there are too few jobs for college graduates? Trying to write on this thesis will produce a poor paper. You have to know what you want to prove before you can prove it, and this student does not know. Yet working as a filing clerk in an office one summer, he learned that the best secretaries were not always the ones with degrees. The ones in the executive position in that office added an innate sense of friendliness to their other qualifications. Therefore, he could write as his thesis statement: A secretary's personality may be more helpful than a degree.

The statement in *b* seems to be two topics: the direction of American education and the bent of many Americans on earning money. It is also too broad. Is all education directed toward financial success? Do all Americans just desire money? Again, this student is hazy about his topic.

Topic *c* does recognize a characteristic of much American education, as is evidenced by history tests requiring many dates or English tests asking for a choice of who or whom. The history teacher who asked his class to study the Bill of Rights and decide whether or not they would be passed today created more lasting learning than the one who asked for a definition of them and the date of their passage. The student might better state the thesis in this way: My education too often consisted in the memorization of facts. Then he could use his past experience as proof.

In *d* we have the vague term "liberal education." Does this mean wide experience or a liberal-arts degree? Certainly we know mature people who have no degree, as well as people whose maturity is respected even though they have been denied education or travel.

The student who wrote *e* must want to write a book. Changes just in the field of English for the last ten years made up a book I recently read. And yet this person says "the American educational system." Such a broad thesis should be reduced to the personal situation, for here the material can come from actual experience. The student might write: The new math made quite a change in my study of arithmetic. Or he could state: It wasn't until I was in the eleventh grade that I found English covered more than grammar.

A thesis statement should suggest no more than the area you can cover in the written paper. For the beginner it should be one which demands no more material than the writer can gain from his own experiences and ideas. If all the class has read some book and discussed it, his topic might, as was said earlier in this chapter, grow out of this discussion.

At times the writer, even as a beginner, may want to investigate further, but this practice, which usually means depending upon encyclopedias for papers, should be discouraged. At first, at least, search your own mind, not the library.

Now, after all this comment, try finding some topic about education you wish to discuss. Write your thesis sentence, keeping it simple and direct. Discuss these statements in class, analyzing them and changing them if necessary.

## B

After creating and discussing the statements for Exercise A-1, you probably realize that such a topic allows for differences of opinion. You may recall that in Chapter One of this book I stated that Plato said rhetoricians must find the truth and then speak, while Aristotle stated that the truth of a situation is not always available and that, therefore, men debate as to the best possible way of dealing with a situation. Men don't debate or argue about the accepted. They debate probabilities: Should this be handled or done in this way?

Think of all the arguments about the Vietnam war. If men had searched longer for the truth of the situation, our troops might never have been there; but, being in, we argued the probability of a military or political solution. Thus it is with all problems. Our feelings, of course, are part of the decision-making process, but these may be influenced by writers and speakers on the subject.

## The Proposition: The Thesis Statement the Writer Must Prove 61

*Exercise* 1

Generally, topics which just explain some situation, whether of the past or the present, are not subjects for persuasive argument. This kind of writing is called exposition. Cookbooks, manuals of how to build (the how-to-do-it books), directions as to how to open a bank account or how to use an appliance, are pure exposition. They do not allow one to take sides. We do, however, find exposition used in argument, as, to prove a point, we may need to explain what the situation or the history of this idea has been. I mention this since at times the emphasis given to exposition may have produced the impression that explanation can never be a part of persuasion. This, of course, is a misconception. To prove the probability the writer suggests in his thesis may include not only explanation but description and narration as well. The main thrust of the persuasive composition, however, is to convince the reader to accept your thesis and to assume that your solution is better than any other.

Write a thesis statement that could come from a discussion of the following situations.

*a.* A young reporter for a radio station wins a prize for a series of broadcasts about pollution problems. As he continues with the subject, he reveals that the eminent citizens of the town are closely connected with the industries causing the most pollution. This time, instead of a prize, he gets fired.

*b.* The family starts out somewhat later than planned on a trip in their car. As the father speeds to make up for lost time, he cautions his two children in the back seat to keep a sharp lookout for a traffic cop.

*c.* Mr. and Mrs. A————, while not college graduates themselves, are pleased that their success in running a motel enables them to send their only son to college. Now, however, they are upset because he has given up the idea of the medical profession and plans to major in drama.

*d.* The college student is not guilty of the traffic violation but decides it is easier to pay the fine than go to court to prove his innocence.

*e.* The high school English teacher complains about her classes. She says the pupils are uninterested and almost defy her to teach them anything.

*Exercise* 2

Write several of the points which might be used for developing one of the thesis statements written for Exercise B-1.

## 62 RHETORICAL TACTICS

*Exercise* 3

Read these thesis statements. How do you think the author plans to develop his speech? (For class discussion.)

But one hundred years later, we must face the tragic fact that the Negro is still not free.—Martin Luther King, Jr., Aug. 28, 1963[1]

So it is apparently necessary for me to state once again—not what kind of church I believe in, for that should be important only to me, but what kind of America I believe in.—John F. Kennedy, Sept. 12, 1960[2]

The clear fact is that the American people must recast their thinking about national problems.—Franklin D. Roosevelt, May 16, 1940[3]

And, if anything, this eighteenth anniversary of the United Nations is an occasion that offers hope.—Adlai Stevenson, Oct. 24, 1963[4]

I say to the House as I said to Ministers who have joined this government, I have nothing to offer but blood, toil, tears, and sweat.—Winston Churchill, May 13, 1940[5]

I submit that the existence in the slums of our large cities of thousands of youths ages 16–21 who are both out-of-school and out-of-work is an explosive situation. It is social dynamite. [There are two sentences here, but the second merely describes in vivid terms the thesis.]—James B. Conant, May 24, 1961[6]

In a famous speech urging imprisonment, not death, for his client, Clarence Darrow, an eminent lawyer, took this as his thesis:

And when the public is interested and demands a punishment, no matter what the offense, great or small, it thinks of only one punishment, and that is death. —Clarence Darrow, 1924[7]

Now, the question for every colored man is, or ought to be, what attitude is assumed by these respective governments and armies towards the rights and liberties of the colored race in this country; which is for us, and which is against us.—Frederick Douglass, July 6, 1863[8]

---

[1] George W. Hibbitt, ed., *The Dolphin Book of Speeches* (Garden City, N.Y.: Doubleday & Co., Inc., 1965), p. 173.
[2] *Ibid.*, p. 179.
[3] *Ibid.*, p. 228.
[4] *Ibid.*, p. 238.
[5] *Ibid.*, p. 281.
[6] *Ibid.*, p. 325.
[7] *Ibid.*, p. 89.
[8] *Ibid.*, p. 167.

CHAPTER SIX

# THE APPEALS: THREE WAYS TO PERSUADE THE READER

To persuade the reader that the author's ideas should be accepted demands more than finding a topic or collecting facts. But this matter of persuasion is not a simple one. It may have been easier in the past when the author spoke to an audience that he knew and when he shared their opinions, their prejudices, their beliefs. He could understand how they would react to his ideas, know that if he presented himself as a good person, made a reasonable argument, won their sympathy, he was quite likely to persuade them.

Our country, however, is not the small city-state of ancient Greece. I know some students, but probably not those in your school; I know my community or my section of it, but not yours; I can perhaps predict the reactions of my age group, but not of yours. Unless I am careful, what seems logical to me may not seem so to you. Even if, instead of writing, I spoke to you over TV, I should still have to persuade through words, although my appearance, voice, and intonation might be helpful in suggesting my sincerity.

Once again, therefore, we turn to Aristotle. As he listened to persuasive speeches, he noted three kinds of appeal to the audience: the rational, the ethical, the emotional. In Greek, they were *logos, ethos,* and *pathos.* While all three are likely to be in one speech, they can be considered separately, and you will find that they can be used in written as well as in oral discourse.

## A

The first appeal was to reason. If man is a rational being, distinguished from other forms of life by his ability to think, then surely he will respond to rational argument. He will also, unfortunately, at times be swayed by irrational or illogical argument.

In this case he allows himself to be distracted from the real issue, much as the sleight of hand artist moves so deftly that the audience doesn't see him palm a coin.

The really good writer does not indulge in tricks. He honestly tries to get his reader to think about what he says, and, after due consideration, to agree with him. At times in the long history of rhetoric, style has been considered the essence of rhetoric, and logic as a separate field of learning. But while style, the wording, the eloquence, does have its own appeal, it cannot replace reason or logic. Thus beginning writers, as well as the beginning students of rhetoric in Aristotle's day, should know a few of the principles of reasoning.

There are, basically, just two methods of reasoning: deductive and inductive. In the first, the argument is based upon an accepted statement which proceeds like this:

Each human being will some day die.
Because I am a human being, I shall some day die.

Frequently people reason from false premises. They see the statistics on juvenile delinquency and take as their premise: "All juvenile delinquents are teen-agers" and then reason: "He is a teen-ager and therefore he is a juvenile delinquent."

Our Declaration of Independence starts with the premise that all men are equal. Thus, when some people refuse to accept the logical reason that since he is a man therefore he is equal to other men, trouble starts.

The beginning writer may know little about the art of deduction, yet he uses it frequently, for circumstantial evidence is a form of deduction. If two cars meet, completely demolishing each other in the crash, it is logical to assume that speed was involved. If the child's face and hands are sticky with cookie crumbs, his mother is quite sure he has had his hands in the cookie jar.

There are, of course, times when circumstantial evidence is incorrect, but people tend to credit it. Examples of this kind of reasoning are found particularly in legal trials. Since, unfortunately, these always seem to be occurring, any student can readily study the use of circumstantial evidence just by reading his daily paper. He may also note, if he reads articles about capital punishment, that aside from the ethical argument that we should never take a human life, its opponents also suggest that, when circumstantial evidence is proved wrong, there is no way of recalling the executed individual back to life.

*Exercise 1*

A mystery story starts with a crime which the detective, professional or amateur, must solve. Think of a story or a film of this kind and prepare to tell the class how the art of deduction was used to find the guilty person.

*Exercise 2*

Relate some experiment from a science class which depends upon deduction.

*Exercise 3*

Bring to class an example of advertising, either from a magazine or TV commercial, which you feel is either based upon a false premise or which distracts from logical reasoning.

Inductive reasoning goes from many examples to a generalization, the formation of a conclusion. Many citizens argue, for example, about unemployment and poverty. Adherents of the proposal for a new method of solving these problems argue that this is a moral obligation; opponents point to the way in which earlier immigrants came to this country and worked their way out of poverty. Often too little explanation is given of the situation, that the man who could get a job digging ditches in grandfather's day now needs to know how to run a bulldozer and that the latter machine can do the work of many spades much more easily and quickly.

In discussing pollution many examples are cited to prove that it must be prevented. We look at the dead fish in many streams and rivers, hear of an Ohio river that is classified as a fire hazard, and state that pollution of our water must be stopped. TV does it by pictures; the writer does it in words.

Sometimes an example might be used for both sides of a question. One writer, to prove our technological skill, might point to successful off-shore drilling for oil. Another might point to the oil leaks which result from this to prove technological advances are often harmful.

One of the most interesting examples of inductive reasoning is that which has been done by linguists, in this case meaning scholars of language, not those who speak several languages. After their study they pointed out that the grammar we have been taught is difficult and unclear because it is describing Latin and not English. Because Latin was admired, earlier educators just applied Latin grammar to English, but it doesn't fit, for English is a word-order language.

Many students fail when asked to define nouns, verbs, adjectives, or adverbs, yet can pick these four parts of speech out of the following nonsense sentence:

Glockly the gloops parted the snarkest drebs.

How can they do this? They do it quite readily by recalling what they have observed in their own speech. They point out these facts:

*The* comes before a noun.
Nouns come before and after verbs.
Verbs can end in *-ed*.
Adverbs often end in *-ly*.
Adjectives often end in *-est* and come between *the* and *the noun*.

There is much more to be learned about our language, but this is the inductive procedure of the linguist: observing how the language works.

*Exercise* 1

Here is a practical exercise in induction. Let everyone in class write a short paragraph about some improvement he feels is needed in his college. Then check the papers and see if you can draw any specific conclusions about these questions.

*a.* Is there any agreement upon improvements? If so, would the percentage of agreement be sufficient to suggest that the whole college desired this change?

*b.* Can you tell from these papers whether spelling errors are frequent? If so, what words caused the most trouble?

*Exercise* 2

Explain how a man like Dr. Salk used the inductive method in producing a serum to prevent polio.

*Exercise* 3

Advertisements often say that "Nine out of ten dentists recommend . . . ." If these figures mean ninety percent of only ten dentists, then they offer scant proof for a nation with many dentists. If they mean ninety percent of

## The Appeals: Three Ways to Persuade the Reader 67

all dentists in the United States, then the statistics are impressive. Until they explain, I think I shall not buy that toothpaste. Bring in an example from advertising which, you feel, uses the inductive method to persuade the viewer to come to a false conclusion.

*Exercise* 4

Sinclair Lewis's novel *Arrowsmith* presents a doctor, who, in an emotional moment, gives everyone, not just a certain group, the injection that will prevent cholera. Schools often use this idea of control groups in reaching a conclusion about certain programs. Businesses take polls to discover whether their product is selling. Write briefly of some inductive experiment of this kind which has come to your attention.

### B

The ethical appeal is centered chiefly in the character presented by the speaker or writer, his ethos. The early rhetoricians felt that the good orator must be a good man, and it is still true that a speaker or writer whom we consider intelligent, well-informed, and sympathetic to our needs and desires probably can persuade us more easily than one we feel is cold or dishonest, no matter how many facts he uses to prove his point.

This kind of appeal causes us to identify ourselves with him, to feel that we will probably agree with or at least think seriously about what he proposes. When one's audience is large and, generally unseen, this poses a problem as any President knows when he plans his Inaugural Address. It posed a particular problem for John F. Kennedy.

He was much younger than the European statesmen, yet he wanted Europeans to recognize that the American president was a man of equal stature. Many had objected to his religion; he had to make these voters feel he would be a good leader. Because speeches are broadcast and printed outside as well as in the country he had to think of how to appeal to this widely various group, some of whom would have to get his ideas from hearing it, others from a more leisurely reading. As a result, Kennedy used an ethical appeal. He established himself as the young but responsible leader determined to carry the nation with him to a better life for all nations. The language was characteristic of what the Greek orators called "the middle style," slightly above the tone of our ordinary speech, yet fairly simple and clear.

You may understand this whole matter of ethos better by examining some introductory paragraphs, for establishing of character should occur early in the speech or article. While shoddy logic may destroy the character as first presented, this early impression is important. There might not be so many volumes of joke books for after-dinner speakers if these men and women, often amateurs at this, did not desire to create good humor and acceptance by their audience.

But the introduction to the Declaration of Independence was most serious. Many people would read this, those in European countries as well as the colonists in America. Careless writing, unwise choice of words could have made these citizens of the New World appear as a bunch of rabble-rousers. Jefferson's skill with language presented instead a young nation that had reluctantly and only from necessity decided to separate from the Mother Country.

### *A Declaration by the Representatives of The United States of America, in General Congress Assembled*

When, in the course of human events, it becomes necessary for one people to dissolve the political bands which have connected them with another, and to assume among the powers of the earth the separate and equal station to which the laws of nature and of Nature's God entitle them, a decent respect to the opinions of mankind requires that they should declare the causes which impel them to the separation.

We hold these truths to be self-evident: that all men are created equal; that they are endowed by their Creator with certain inalienable rights; that among these are life, liberty, and the pursuit of happiness; that to secure these rights, governments are instituted among men, deriving their just powers from the consent of the governed; that whenever any form of government becomes destructive of these ends, it is the right of the people to alter or abolish it, and to institute new government, laying its foundation on such principles, and organizing its powers in such form, as to them shall seem most likely to effect their safety and happiness. Prudence, indeed, will dictate that governments long established should not be changed for light and transient causes; and accordingly all experience hath shown that mankind are more disposed to suffer while evils are sufferable, than to right themselves by abolishing the forms to which they are accustomed. But when a long train of abuses and usurpations, pursuing invariably the same object, evinces a design to reduce them under absolute despotism, it is their right, it is their duty to throw off such government, and to provide new guards for their future security. Such has been the patient sufferance of these colonies; and such is now the necessity which constrains them to alter their former systems of government. The history of the present king of Great Britain is a history of repeated injuries and usurpations, all having in direct object the establishment of an absolute tyranny over these states. To prove this, let facts be submitted to a candid world.

A second example of ethos comes from an article written by a college student in 1970. What kind of person does this paragraph reveal?

### An End to Our National Ego[1]

The complacent 1950's and early 60's are gone. Joe College has been replaced by activists who call for a redistribution of wealth, a commitment to racial justice and a remaking of educational policies. Working with blacks in the civil rights struggle, young white Americans grow sensitive to inequities around them. Military spending and the Vietnam War have further convinced students that national priorities are as polluted as the air in our cities. Students all over America are turning in their social calendars for their social responsibilities. Incredible that this should frighten the rest of America rather than encourage her.

A third example comes from a book entitled *Compulsory Mis-education* by Paul Goodman.[2] In the first paragraph of the preface he certainly doesn't seem to be presenting himself as a popular character. Would you feel, after reading this, like trusting his ideas? If so, why? If not, why?

In these remarks on the schools, I do not try to be generous or fair, but I have seen what I am talking about and I hope I am rational. This case is that we have been swept on a flood-tide of public policy and popular

---

[1] Daniel Pellegrom, "An End to Our National Ego," *AAUW Journal* (May, 1970), p. 170.
[2] Paul Goodman, *Compulsory Mis-education and The Community of Scholars* (Vintage Book; New York: Random House, 1964), p. 7.

sentiment into an expansion of schooling and an aggrandizement of schoolpeople that is grossly wasteful of wealth and effort and does positive damage to the young. Yet I do not hear any fundamental opposition in principle, nor even prudent people (rather than stingy people) saying, go warily. The dominance of the present school auspices prevents any new thinking about education, although we face unprecedented conditions.

Another example comes from a magazine, *The New Yorker*,[3] which reprinted a speech Mr. Wald, a professor of biology at Harvard, made to an audience of scientists assembled at the Massachusetts Institute of Technology on March 4, 1969. After reading his introduction, do you think that Mr. Wald can speak truly about the problem of student unrest? His title was "A Generation in Search of a Future."

All of you know that in the last couple of years there has been student unrest, breaking at times into violence, in many parts of the world: in England, Germany, Italy, Spain, Mexico, Japan, and, needless to say, many parts of this country. There has been a great deal of discussion as to what it all means. Perfectly clearly, it means something different in Mexico from what it does in France, and something different in France from what it does in Tokyo, and something different in Tokyo from what it does in this country. Yet, unless we are to assume that students have gone crazy all over the world, or that they have just decided that it's the thing to do, it must have some common meaning.

I don't need to go so far afield to look for that meaning. I am a teacher, and at Harvard I have a class of about three hundred and fifty students— men and women—most of them freshmen and sophomores. Over these past few years, I have felt increasingly that something is terribly wrong—and this year ever so much more than last. Something has gone sour, in teaching and in learning. It's almost as though there were a widespread feeling that education has become irrelevant.

A lecture is much more of a dialogue than many of you probably realize. As you lecture, you keep watching the faces, and information keeps coming back to you all the time. I began to feel, particularly this year, that I was missing much of what was coming back. I tried asking the students, but they didn't or couldn't help me very much.

[3] *The New Yorker*, March 22, 1969, Notes & Comment.

But I think I know what's the matter. I think that this whole generation of students is beset with a profound uneasiness, and I don't think that they have yet quite defined its source. I think I understand the reasons for their uneasiness even better than they do. What is more, I share their uneasiness.

*Exercise 1*

On the stage, TV, or film we may see a person who has built for himself a certain kind of character. This may be a matter which the actor must work out for himself, as is shown in the following passage, where Dick Gregory[4] concludes that "Comedy is friendly relations."

After reading this quotation, write a paragraph in which you show how some comedian you have seen works at creating a character which establishes these friendly relations."

Some day I'm going to be performing where the bread is, in the big white night clubs. When I step up on that stage, in *their* neighborhood, some of them are going to feel sorry for me because I'm a Negro, and some of them are going to hate me because I'm a Negro. Those who feel sorry might laugh a little at first. But they can't respect someone they pity, and eventually they'll stop laughing. Those who hate me aren't going to laugh at all.

I've got to hit them fast, before they can think, just the way I hit those kids back in St. Louis who picked on me because I was raggedy and had no Daddy. I've got to go up there as an individual first, a Negro second. I've got to be a colored funny man, not a funny colored man. I've got to act like a star who isn't sorry for himself—that way, they can't feel sorry for me. I've got to make jokes about myself, before I can make jokes about them and their society—that way, they can't hate me. Comedy is friendly relations.

*Exercise 2*

The phrase, so one read, used by college students who worked for Senator Eugene McCarthy was "Clean for Gene." While surface appearance might be more appealing as they visited with older voters, what other qualities must they have had to be effective?

*Exercise 3*

In convocations on the campus, in lecture halls, and on TV we hear speakers. After listening to one, write your impression of the speaker's character.

---

[4] Dick Gregory, *Nigger* (New York: E. P. Dutton & Co., Inc., 1964), pp. 147–148.

*Exercise* 4

A book published in 1969 was entitled *The Selling of the President.* Since a college student has had some years of watching TV, he should be able to discuss whether or not a political candidate can be built up as successfully as a new detergent. What is your opinion? Support your idea with examples from your own experience in TV viewing.

# C

The third and last method of appeal was the emotional one. Aristotle was not a psychologist, yet he recognized that the speaker who understood emotional qualities, understood his audience sufficiently to know what would arouse them and how this could be done, stood a better chance of making an effective speech than the man who made scant appeal to the feelings of his audience.

A modern student, although he is not a psychologist either, should understand how he can affect the emotions of others and, also, how others may affect him. For in this era of mass communication he is exposed every day to an appeal to his emotions. Having lived with TV commercials during his lifetime, he is probably skeptical about much of this, realizing that no deodorant or mouthwash will make up for a bad disposition. There are, however, many times when the appeal is less obvious, and then we need to think before we casually accept what is said or suggested.

In the classical era this emotional appeal (The name given it was *pathos*.) occurred at the ending of the speech, the peroration. It was likely to be phrased in an elegant manner, the high style. Perhaps, again, we can understand better by reading examples.

The first one comes from a famous speech by Patrick Henry.[5] This was his final paragraph.

It is in vain, sir, to extenuate the matter. Gentlemen may cry peace, peace—but there is no peace. The war is actually begun! The next gale that sweeps from the north will bring to our ears the clash of resounding arms! Our brethren are already in the field! Why stand we here idle? What is it that gentlemen wish? What would they have? Is life so dear, or peace so sweet, as to be purchased at the price of chains and slavery? Forbid it,

---

[5] Patrick Henry, "Give Me Liberty, or Give Me Death!" *The Dolphin Book of Speeches,* edited by George W. Hibbitt (Garden City, N.Y.: Doubleday & Company, Inc., 1965), p. 154.

Almighty God! I know not what course others may take; but as for me, give me liberty, or give me death!

Here is the conclusion of Black Hawk's speech to General Street.[6] Notice how he appeals to the love of family, friends, and country. How else does he arouse sympathy?

Black Hawk is a true Indian, and disdains to cry like a woman. He feels for his wife, his children, and his friends. But he does not care for himself. He cares for the Nation and the Indians. They will suffer. He laments their Fate. Farewell, my Nation! Black Hawk tried to save you, and avenge your wrongs. He drank the blood of some of the whites. He has been taken prisoner, and his plans are crushed. He can do no more. He is near his end. His sun is setting, and he will rise no more. Farewell to Black Hawk.

But such fervent appeals are not likely to be needed in the usual composition. You need the ordinary incident, one the reader relates to his own life. Read the twenty-third Psalm and notice how this writer of long ago used terms which would be appreciated by a nomadic people who herded flocks in desert areas. Here the Lord is the "shepherd" with his "rod and staff." Grass for the flocks was important, so man is led to "green pastures" and beside "still waters," even more important in arid country.

In modern times advertisers use this kind of appeal to sell their products. Our rivers and streams are filled with suds as women buy detergents, for the housewife does want to wash clothes clean. And while advertisers seem to exploit this kind of persuasion, it can be used honestly. Urging other young people to help you work to procure a recreation center will be more successful if you suggest the pleasure and fun it will give them. But this might not convince the city administrators. They would be more likely to listen if you suggested how this center could help solve some of their problems with young people.

Another example of a simple appeal is in "A Fable for Tomorrow," the first chapter of Rachel Carson's *Silent Spring*. Read this and then list the various emotions she arouses, remembering of course,

---

[6] William Jennings Bryan, ed., *The World's Famous Orations*, Vol. VIII (New York: Funk & Wagnalls Company, 1906), p. 23.

that many of the generation to whom she directed this had memories of the countryside she describes.

## A Fable for Tomorrow[7]

There was once a town in the heart of America where all life seemed to live in harmony with its surroundings. The town lay in the midst of a checkerboard of prosperous farms, with fields of grain and hillsides of orchards where, in spring, white clouds of bloom drifted above the green fields. In autumn, oak and maple and birch set up a blaze of color that flamed and flickered across a backdrop of pines. Then foxes barked in the hills and deer silently crossed the fields, half hidden in the mists of the fall mornings.

Along the roads, laurel, viburnum and alder, great ferns and wildflowers delighted the traveler's eye through much of the year. Even in winter the roadsides were places of beauty, where countless birds came to feed on the berries and on the seed heads of the dried weeds rising above the snow. The countryside was, in fact, famous for the abundance and variety of its bird life, and when the flood of migrants was pouring through in spring and fall people traveled from great distances to observe them. Others came to fish the streams, which flowed clear and cold out of the hills and contained shady pools where trout lay. So it had been from the days many years ago when the first settlers raised their houses, sank their wells, and built their barns.

Then a strange blight crept over the area and everything began to change. Some evil spell had settled on the community: mysterious maladies swept the flocks of chickens; the cattle and sheep sickened and died. Everywhere was a shadow of death. The farmers spoke of much illness among their families. In the town the doctors had become more and more puzzled by new kinds of sickness appearing among their patients. There had been several sudden and unexplained deaths, not only among adults but even among children, who would be stricken suddenly while at play and die within a few hours.

There was a strange stillness. The birds, for example—where had they gone? Many people spoke of them, puzzled and disturbed. The feeding stations in the backyards were deserted. The few birds seen anywhere

---

[7] Rachel Carson, "A Fable for Tomorrow," *Silent Spring* (A Fawcett Crest Book; Greenwich, Conn.: Fawcett Publications, Inc., 1966), pp. 13–15.

were moribund; they trembled violently and could not fly. It was a spring without voices. On the mornings that had once throbbed with the dawn chorus of robins, catbirds, doves, jays, wrens, and scores of other bird voices there was now no sound; only silence lay over the fields and woods and marsh.

On the farms the hens brooded, but no chicks hatched. The farmers complained that they were unable to raise any pigs—the litters were small and the young survived only a few days. The apple trees were coming into bloom but no bees droned among the blossoms, so there was no pollination and there would be no fruit.

The roadsides, once so attractive, were now lined with browned and withered vegetation as though swept by fire. These, too, were silent, deserted by all living things. Even the streams were now lifeless. Anglers no longer visited them, for all the fish had died.

In the gutters under the eaves and between the shingles of the roofs, a white granular powder still showed a few patches; some weeks before it had fallen like snow upon the roofs and the lawns, the fields and streams.

No witchcraft, no enemy action had silenced the rebirth of new life in this stricken world. The people had done it themselves.

This town does not actually exist, but it might easily have a thousand counterparts in America or elsewhere in the world. I know of no community that has experienced all the misfortunes I describe. Yet every one of these disasters has actually happened somewhere, and many real communities have already suffered a substantial number of them. A grim specter has crept upon us almost unnoticed, and this imagined tragedy may easily become a stark reality we all shall know.

What has already silenced the voices of spring in countless towns in America? This book is an attempt to explain.

*Exercise* 1

You wish to explain to a friend that he is being flattered or praised into making the wrong decision. What incident from experiences you have had could you use to show him his mistake?

*Exercise* 2

We all, to use the old saying, "Act in haste, repent in leisure." What incident from your life could you tell a friend that might make him act more carefully? Remember, this kind of appeal means that the listener must sense that the experience is one that could also happen to him.

*Exercise 3*

Listen carefully to some speech, whether on TV or by some lecturer on campus, and write a brief paragraph analyzing his use of incidents for emotional appeal.

*Exercise 4*

Discussion usually precedes a strike. Suppose you and your class are all dissatisfied workers. Decide who your employer is and what your grievances are. Perhaps you work for a hospital or a large hotel. Then hold a mass meeting to decide whether or not to strike. Various points of view may be presented: the demand for an instant strike, the feeling that peaceful negotiation is better, the idea that a low salary is better than no salary, the feeling that strike action will offend the public. Assume the role of a person from one of these groups (you may think of others) and discuss the situation. Then take a vote as to whether or not to strike.

Afterwards, in your regular role of student, discuss what appeal made you vote as you did.

*Exercise 5*

Richard J. Barnet is discussing the amount of money spent on defense. In this quotation, to what emotion does he imply the defense department appeals?

Every new weapons system has been presented to the public doubly wrapped: an inside wrapping of baffling technical detail, and, on the outside, the flag.

Why would this appeal be used?

*Exercise 6*

In the following situations the writer could use more than one way to appeal to the reader. Choose three of the following situations and then explain how you could persuade the reader to accept your idea on the subject.

*a.* Get an outside group to make a contribution to some campus activity.

*b.* Persuade an instructor to give you another chance on a quiz you missed taking.

*c.* Plan an approach to the city council urging the need for a traffic light at a specific corner.

*d.* Convince an employer to overlook your inexperience in hiring you.

*e.* Explain to a company or store why they should refund the purchase price of a defective piece of merchandise.

*f.* A college has a strongly parental attitude about student behavior. Convince the Dean of Women, hitherto a supporter of the Administration point of view, that more freedom is justified.

*g.* A boy's uncle is greatly disturbed because his nephew went to college, thus evading the draft. Defend the boy's action.

*h.* The job you desire seems unattainable because of union requirements for that kind of work. Try to explain to one of the union members why this should be changed.

*i.* Explain to parents who wished a college career for their child why the boy or girl feels college is unnecessary.

CHAPTER SEVEN

# THE TOPICS: FINDING OUT WHAT YOU KNOW ABOUT A SUBJECT

Discussion of a subject in or out of class not only helps you discover your thesis statement but also provides points to prove it, particularly if the subject deals with a fictional character or situation, for here the fiction itself supplies sufficient examples to prove a thesis. But when the discussion is based upon current happenings, problems about which you have heard or read, you may add to the information gathered from these sources your own observations and experiences. In fact, the substance of the entire composition may, at times, be derived entirely from experiences in the writer's life. This would seem to make the task of composition easier but in reality it doesn't, for the mind never seems to file ideas and experiences in neat order. Instead, minds are rather like the old-fashioned attic or the storeroom, a jumble of discards no longer used and apparently forgotten. There may be as much confusion as in the junk-yard or second-hand shop, but at least their wares are set out before you, making the search for the item you desire simpler. The mind just doesn't do this. You have to ask it questions to find out what is there.

### A

The ancient teachers called these questions the "common topics," and they dealt with definition, comparison, relationship, circumstances, and testimony. Not all five will always apply, but even if only two or three resurrect ideas, the results may be sufficient to complete a couple of pages, enough for a short composition.

(To prevent confusion, it might be well to explain here the different uses of the word *topic*. It frequently refers to the general subject matter of a speech or composition: He will discuss this *topic*. The term is also used in connection with the point to be discussed in a paragraph: This is the *topic* sentence for the first paragraph. In this chapter the *topics,* although they can be discussed one at a time, is a rhetorical term, referring to those questions which an individual can use as a guide or check list to find out what he knows about his subject.)

1. *Definition* to students accustomed to being told to look up the meaning in the dictionary means a quotation from one, but to use this quotation as the beginning sentence for a composition is comparable to the use of "well" at the beginning of an oral statement and quite as ineffective. Just as the word "well" creates uncertainty about the answer or statement, so the quoted definition reveals the writer's uncertainty as to how to begin, especially when the reader accepts the quoted definition of the term. But if you as the writer use a term which carries a personal meaning, you must define this term for your reader. And you should always remember that the true meaning of a word is the way in which the reader will interpret it. Writing directed toward your own group or class, therefore, simplifies this problem.

Another way to define is to explain to what division the subject belongs. Each year the Congress debates foreign aid and citizens argue about it, frequently with no real knowledge of what is involved. The bill might cover agricultural aid; it might be for military assistance; it could cover both. Argument might be more reasonable if divisions were clear. Again, controversy over the penalties for the use of marijuana might be lessened when it is definitely decided as to what class of drugs marijuana belongs. If a student states that traffic fatalities should be decreased, his reader may wonder whether he is referring to those caused by careless drivers or those caused by structural defects in cars. After Rachel Carson's *Silent Spring,* it is difficult to argue that the use of insecticides increases agricultural production without explaining that the ones you suggest are not harmful to mankind.

Perhaps the writer will need to define the kind of subject he has in mind. If he writes that he believes in a democracy, more than a dictionary definition of the word must be given, for the democracy of today is not like that of the city-state of Greece or the town meeting of early New England. In the process of defining his kind of democracy, the student makes the subject clearer to the reader, but what is even more important, out of all his hazy ideas he clarifies and defines his own subject and thesis. Therefore, before rushing off to consult Webster's when you are thinking about your composition ask: Is definition necessary and, if so, what kind of definition?

2. *Comparison* may be simple, like telling a child that the world is round like an orange, for explaining the unknown by reference to a similarity in the known assists in clarification of an idea or concept. Or you can show a difference, explaining that what the boy did was only a prank in a sparsely settled rural America but a crime in a more urban and populous country. There may be a difference in degree. The student in Chapter Five of this book, who decided that cafeteria prices were going to be too high, might argue instead for their acceptance, suggesting that considering the rate of inflation the new price was considerably less than it might have been.

3. *Relationship,* the third topic, always suggests some sort of connection, often a cause-and-effect situation. Ancient peoples, observing the rising and setting of the sun, made up stories to account for this. When there is an effect there should be, so the reader will feel, a cause. This may demand a bit of exploration on your part as you seek the cause.

For example, many older students are not very good readers. I could blame the students but in my work I had an opportunity to see what went on in the elementary grades. There I found that many teachers used nothing but Dick and Jane, a visual method. Perhaps this was at least partly the cause for some poor readers, and if I had planned a composition my thesis statement might have been: Elementary teachers need to know more than one method for teaching reading. But I shall probably have to have much more evidence to convince some educators. These cause-and-effect arguments do, however, lend themselves to error. Not all bad luck can be attributed to walking under a ladder.

Another kind of relationship is shown when, for instance, a teacher looking at the past failures on a student's record, automatically assumes he will fail this year. The consequence of past failure need not be failure again. A further example is shown in the action of legislators who limit the funding of their state university as a consequence of campus disturbances.

4. *Circumstance,* the fourth topic, may be a way of persuading the sceptical person that the impossible is possible. Achieving an America free of pollution sounds like an impossible task at this time, but so was the idea earlier of reaching the moon. Surely if all the skill, the technology, and the money formerly devoted to space were now spent on the problem of pollution, it would be possible once more to have clean air and clean water. The student who hunts up another garage because the mechanic at one never seemed to repair his car does so because he feels that what has happened in the past can happen in the future. Poor workmanship in the past indicates to him poor workmanship on future occasions.

5. The fifth and last topic is that of *authority.* In law courts, lawyers speak of precedents, going back to decisions in previous cases. Bringing up new cases to the courts, establishing new precedents, is one way of creating change. Laws themselves establish authority.

A frequent example of authority is the testimonial. If the athletic hero eats this kind of cereal, then all would-be heroes will eat it. TV programs are lost because of the Nielson rating, what a sampling of people thinks of the show.

At the risk of boring the reader, the writer uses statistics, charts, and graphs. This can be useful, but a book entitled *How to Lie with Statistics,* would seem to warn the reader to be careful of his acceptance of all figures.

We even use old proverbs to prove our point, admonishing young people that "Haste makes waste."

Suppose I use the topics to find out what I can say about this proposition: My city should run its own bus service. I agree that this is not an exciting topic. Many details of daily life are not, but if you took the bus, as I do, then the subject would be meaningful to you as well as to other bus-riders. And if I find the facts I need and state them in words which picture the need for change, then perhaps instead of an apathetic group of citizens deploring the lack of service, they will join me in demanding something better.

Now our city has, at present, two kinds of buses, the big ramshackle ones which an outstate company has the franchise to run, and the mini-buses, compact little affairs which the merchants purchased for the use of people in the central shopping area. Their fares differ.

Thus, while *bus* need not be defined, the question of definition reminds me that I had better explain the two kinds, since the purpose of my paper is to urge that the city council cancel only the franchise of the outstate company.

When it comes to comparison, I find there is much material. I can compare the comfort of the mini-buses with the discomfort of the larger ones, compare the punctuality of the one with the erratic schedule of the other. I can also discuss the deterioration of service, describing what it once was and what it is now.

Relationship brings to mind our traffic problems. While driving one's own car to work seems to be an American custom, declining bus service makes this even more necessary, adding to this traffic problem. Besides, when fewer people ride the bus, profits are less. Thus the company neglects repairs, curtails routes, and underpays its drivers. Strikes are a frequent threat.

The question of circumstance makes me think again of the mini-bus. This I understand (testimony from newspaper articles) has been a profitable operation. If this could be done for the shopping area, couldn't something like this be done for the whole city?

Additional testimony as to the quality of city ownership comes from old residents who state the company has not lived up to the conditions set when the franchise was granted.

In this case, all five questions recall ideas I have on the subject. Expansion is needed, but my paper is well begun.

*Exercise* 1

When Burke gave his famous speech on "Conciliation with the Colonies," he used some of these ideas. Which of the topics do you think he was using?

*a.* Trade, development of the land, and increase of population are making the American colonies wealthy and they are more likely to share this wealth if they remain a part of the mother country.

*b.* Force will not be helpful because the colonists are really Englishmen who have been brought up in freedom.

*c.* Representation in Parliament has been given to Wales, Chester, and Durham, and therefore can be given to the colonies.

*d.* Force is useless, for how can it be maintained at so great a distance?

## Exercise 2

What reasoning lies behind statements like these?
a. This costs too much.
b. That's a foolish thing to do.
c. Be careful in choosing your friends.
d. He's a liar.
e. I could have told you this would happen.

## Exercise 3

W. E. DuBois[1] in discussing the meaning of progress begins with a description of the school where he first taught. This enables his reader to appreciate the changes he mentions when he returns to the scene ten years later. He writes:

> The schoolhouse was a log hut, where Colonel Wheeler used to shelter his corn. It sat in a lot behind a rail fence and thorn bushes, near the sweetest of springs. There was an entrance where a door once was, and within, a massive rickety fireplace; great chinks between the logs served as windows. Furniture was scarce. A pale blackboard crouched in the corner. My desk was made of three boards, reinforced at critical points, and my chair, borrowed from the landlady, had to be returned every night. Seats for the children—these puzzled me much. I was haunted by a New England vision of neat little desks and chairs, but, alas! the reality was rough plank benches without backs, and at times without legs. They had the one virtue of making naps dangerous,—possibly fatal, for the floor was not to be trusted.

Now suppose you want to show the nature of progress in your area. Is life there more or less agreeable today? Is it strange to you now? Do the old neighbors seem happier or are they no longer there? Is there a new school or still the same old brick structure? Is a once quiet street now filled with constant traffic? Does a new factory pollute the atmosphere? The topic of comparison should help you decide whether what you remember and what you see now will persuade your reader that the nature of progress here is for the better or for the worse. In your case, since yours is not to be a long paper, you could put the comparison of the scene as it was and as it is now in one paragraph. Write your example.

---

[1] W. E. DuBois, *The Souls of Black Folk* (Greenwich, Conn.: Fawcett Publications, Inc., 1961), p. 57.

*Exercise* 4

A man is shown to be a capable individual by comparison with another considered equally capable. The Greeks, so close to the sea, often compared a leader with a successful captain of a ship. He steered the ship past reefs. He saw that the sails were trimmed. He concerned himself with the weather. He could tell directions from the stars.

Today you might compare our successful character to an astronaut. What virtues can you list?

*a.* He takes care of his health.
*b.* He studies every problem.
*c.* He practices using all the equipment until he really knows how.
*d.* He follows directions.
*e.* He does not panic.
*f.* He is courageous.

Try to put all such details into a paragraph comparing a self-reliant boy to an astronaut or to any other professional who needs such traits.

*Exercise* 5

Erasmus[2] translated the following paragraph (today we might divide it into two) that Quintilian gave as an example to the students of his day of the way the writer can expand a topic sentence by piling up comparisons. To make doubly sure his topic sentence is remembered, notice that he also uses it as his last sentence.

A wise man will shun no peril in the service of his country. Because it often happens that he who has been unwilling to die for his country necessarily perishes with it. And since every advantage has been accepted from his country, no disadvantage ought to be considered grievous in its service. Therefore, they who flee the peril that they ought to undergo in the service of their country act foolishly. For they are unable to escape it and are discovered to be ungrateful to the state. But those who at their own peril fend off the perils of their fatherland are to be deemed wise, since they render to the Republic the honor they owe it, and prefer to die in defense of many rather than with many. For it is extremely unjust when you have preserved with the help of your country the life you received from nature, to render that life to nature when she requires it and not to give it to your country when she requests it, and when you are able with the greatest virtue and honor to die for your country,

---

[2] Desiderius Erasmus, *On Copia of Words and Ideas,* translated by Donald B. King and H. David Rix (Milwaukee, Wisc.: Marquette University Press, 1963), pp. 83–84.

## The Topics: Finding Out What You Know About a Subject

to prefer to live through dishonor and cowardice, and although you are willing to expose yourself to peril in defense of friends, parents, and other relatives, to be unwilling to go into danger in defense of your country in which both they and that most sacred name of fatherland are included. And, just as he ought to be despised who in sailing puts his own safety above that of his ship, so he ought to be censured who in his country's danger consults his own rather than common safety. Many people have been saved from shipwreck; no one is able to swim away safely from the wreck of his own country. [Here he gives an example from Greek history.] And Decius, who is said to have sacrificed himself in behalf of the legions by throwing himself into the midst of the enemy seems to have understood this. Because he gave up his life he did not perish. For he bought the noblest thing with the commonest; he gave his life and received his country. Losing his life, he gained glory that, prolonged by age with the highest praise, becomes brighter every day. Now if it has been demonstrated by reason and confirmed by example that one ought to undergo danger in defense of his country, those ought to be considered wise who shun no peril in defense of their country's safety.

These ideas are still, despite the centuries that have intervened, like the ones of those who support the draft today. But suppose you are one of the youthful objectors. Write an expanded paragraph proving that you are not "shunning peril in the service of your country."

*Exercise 6*

Write a paragraph that tells the reader how happy (or unhappy) you are. Follow this pattern.

1. Write a topic sentence.
2. Follow with a restatement, although in different words, of this idea.
3. Compare your present state with previous ones of this kind. Is this worse or better?
4. Contrast your happiness or unhappiness with the opposite emotion.
5. Give an example of someone in the past or in the outside world whose happiness or unhappiness must be like this state of yours.

*Exercise 7*

A person may pay little attention to a subject, even though it may concern him or his way of life, because he feels he knows little about it and hasn't the time for investigation. Nevertheless he may know more than he realizes. Choose some subject about which you feel your knowledge is slight and then, by use of the "common topics" list the facts you find you do know.

## B

Then there were the special topics, fewer in number and differing according to the kind of discourse to be composed. In a way, they determine the atmosphere of the composition.

Although as students you may have little reason to compose a formal ceremonial or judicial speech, you are certainly exposed to them. Each evening, if you listen to the news on ABC-TV, you have heard the broadcast close with a short speech, a judgment on some phase of American life or government. And I doubt if a day goes by without your making some kind of judgment in your own conversation. Perhaps you listen less to the ceremonial speech, but these too are printed or heard on TV. Under these circumstances, you should understand the special topic which governs each, the ceremonial and the judicial.

In the ceremonial discourse, the topic was that of praise or blame, probably with the underlying feeling that the reader or listener should profit from this listing of virtues or vices, and thereafter either emulate the virtue or avoid the sin. These virtues or vices may not be the same in every case. The man who won the Nobel prize for producing a strain of wheat which will increase food production will hardly be praised in the same way as the winner of a gold medal in the Olympics. The first is commended for his knowledge, skill, and diligence; the athlete for his physical prowess, courage and good sportsmanship.

Sometimes this emphasis upon virtue seems to be carried to excess in "the man who" speeches at political conventions, where the listing of virtues makes the individual sound like Superman. And your decisions as to what to praise or blame the person or event for may change according to your age and the age in which you live. Even if you are not writing this kind of material yourself, you should at least understand its organization and purpose, since it is quite possible that at times the person or event is not one which truly merits praise. Neither may the person or event merit the comments which condemn.

*Exercise* 1

The following situations will not produce formal ceremonial discourses, but they are the kind students may write. Try to do one of the three.

*a.* Suppose a person whom you like and admire dies. Since you knew him well, you are asked to write a paragraph about him for the school paper.

*b.* Your school is beginning an evaluation of its teachers and asks for student opinion. There is space on the page for a short paragraph. Your name need not be included. Try writing one for a teacher you dislike or have disliked.

*c.* You are asked to present a gift to a friend who is moving away. He has been liked by the whole group, particularly because he has helped all of your group at various times. Write what you would say.

Since the Greek citizen often represented himself in legal circumstances, he may have needed the topics for judicial discourse more than we do, for we hire lawyers. There are times, however, when we wish to take issue with other opinions, condemn another's actions, or defend our own actions. Under these circumstances it is well to know the special topics relating to judicial discourse.

These are justice or injustice, but they cannot be considered until the questions of fact, definition, and quality have been settled. These, as you will recall from Chapter Five, were questions also used in determining your proposition.

Fact is discovered by evidence, but the kind and reliability of the evidence must be established. Witnesses can be mistaken. A man known to be a liar is likely to have his evidence discounted. Defining the situation means knowing what particular law was violated and what was the effect of this violation. The third was quality, which discusses the ideas of motive, extenuating circumstances, the kind of person who broke the law. Only after all this can the special topics of justice or injustice be considered. If the thief was seen, if he stole for personal gain, his punishment is considered as just. If, however, he is a poor man who stole bread for his starving children, the same penalty as given the first thief might be considered unjust.

*Exercise* 1

Bring to class a newspaper report of some case. Examine the evidence given, the definition of the case, and then its quality. After this is settled you can consider the topics of justice or injustice in relation to the case.

*Exercise* 2

Mrs. A―――, a widow, has difficulty in supervising her children because she works all day. Now her son, a student in junior high, has again been accused of petty theft. The authorities suggest he be put in a foster home. His mother objects. Present the case and have class members give speeches for or against this suggestion or any others that might be made.

*Exercise 3*

The terms "justice" and "injustice" have been used as special topics. You have been using them in both Exercises 1 and 2. Write your definition of these terms.

The special topics for deliberative discourse, the kind that most concerns us, were two. The first is an appeal to the worth or good of an idea, a moral or ethical value. The second is an appeal to the usefulness or expediency of a proposition, what it is advantageous to do. Both topics imply, however, that the reader or listener will be a happier or more satisfied person if he accepts the author's solution to a problem.

The choice of topics, whether we shall use the good or the advantageous, depends upon the nature of our subject and the nature of our audience. Although we have the old saying that "Cleanliness is next to godliness," firms do not use the topic of worth in advertising detergents. When Durward Kirby reaches for his particular brand of detergent in the supermarket, telling the two housewives he always chooses it, he does not persuade them to pay the few extra cents it costs by telling them this is a good or worthy act. He tells them they can wash more dishes with this detergent than with the cheaper brand. They can save money and, an appeal to feminine vanity, have smoother hands.

The special topics of both the good and the advantageous are used in arguments about poverty in our nation, with some citizens stating that elimination of poverty is the only just or good thing to do. Others, however, argue from expediency: if there is no poverty, if every man has a job, prosperity will increase which will result in a richer nation.

The special topic of the worthy and the good was used at first about the war in Vietnam. It was only good to help the South Vietnamese against communism. Then, as the war was prolonged, the topic of expediency took over: too much money went to the war.

The flight of Apollo 11 brought the special topics into use. Some articles praised it as a glorious example of man's ability; others suggested this earth needed the same effort and money.

In daily life people argue between the worthy and the expedient almost unconsciously. In a period of inflation, supermarkets are filled with women staring at the meat counter, trying to decide whether hamburger or stewing beef is better for the budget. Because, over all, the housewife does care for her family, she consoles herself for buying the cheapest by thinking of a more appetizing way to serve it.

*Exercise 1*
Life insurance companies urge the purchase of policies because a good man cares for his family's welfare. Some cars are advertised as being the best buy for the least money.
Check five TV commercials. Do they appeal to the worthy or to the advantageous?

*Exercise 2*
Which special topic, or it might be the use of both, could be observed in these decisions concerning high school incidents?

*a.* The high school principal foregoes the three-day suspension. Any student who is obviously making no effort and proves troublesome is out for the semester.

*b.* The English department offered students a wide choice of mini-courses, covering a three-week period at the end of the semester and subject only to a pass-fail requirement for credit. The response was so favorable that the administrators will permit this to continue each year.

*c.* The school principal urged a new course in vocational training, but the board members instituted instead a program for wrestling.

*d.* Members of the student council had their petition, requesting the privilege of being granted more responsibility in the conduct of student affairs, denied by the administration.

*e.* Since there are comparatively few students for a third-year language class, the school decides to offer only two years of the language.

*Note:* Now I doubt if you will faithfully go through the list of topics for every paper you write. In fact, I know you won't. But this practice with them in just a few exercises will make them familiar to you, to such an extent that while you will not consciously question, "Now what about comparison or testimony?" you will retain some idea of how to fish around in that cluttered mind to find your material.

CHAPTER EIGHT

# THREE KINDS OF RHETORICAL DISCOURSE

### The Ceremonial Speech

No Fourth of July was complete in the nineteenth century without noisy firecrackers and a patriotic speech. The firecrackers were often dangerous and the speeches pretty dull, but people were happy. Their declaration of independence had been reaffirmed once more.

It was a great day too when the cornerstone was laid for the new post office, and the mayor and local dignitaries spoke in honor of the occasion. At other times the event was a sad one, the church filled with mourners listening to a eulogy, that speech paying tribute to the virtues of the departed citizen.

The voice of the patriotic speaker booms less in this age of microphones, but ceremonial speeches still continue. Men celebrate national achievements, presidents give inaugural addresses, and, when a leader dies, many speak or write of his value to the nation. Perhaps you recall the speeches in late years which praised those who died after long service to their country and those who died before they could accomplish all they had hoped to do.

One of the best known of the ceremonial speeches is Lincoln's Gettysburg address. Its quality has given it a timelessness not all speeches achieve, and yet Lincoln was considered an uneducated man. But he had read Blackstone on law, from which he may have derived the sense of logic, the King James version of the Bible with the rhythm of its sentences, and a book about classical rhetoric. Perhaps all of these helped him write as he did.

We are not yet ready for a complete speech of this nature, but some preliminary work can be done.

*Exercise 1*

Suppose that the astronauts of Apollo 13 had not returned safely to earth. Write a sentence in which you praise them, including adjectives which show this. Then think of a few sentences which extol or praise their adventure. Lastly, think of a sentence or two which tells what their adventure and their loss means to the American people.

*Exercise 2*

Think of someone who has done something you admire. Write a paragraph of praise, giving his virtues, discussing his deed, indicating what he has meant to you or to you and your friends.

**Speeches in Court**

The most important kind of rhetorical speech originally was the judicial one, the forensic. Here was a debate over some past action, one advocate attacking and the other defending his client.

Although Aristotle was not a psychologist, he considered what we might call the psychological factors: the reason for wrong doing, what was wrong, its effect on others. (Did the person steal because his family was starving or did he do it because it was nice to get free bread and the baker would not miss it?) He also realized that court trials meant a study and interpretation of laws.

All of this doesn't sound much like the old Perry Mason courtroom on TV, and it isn't. Neither does it sound much like our overcrowded courts of today, where, as I understand, there is a practice of letting the individual plead guilty, perhaps for a lesser sentence, foregoing a trial with its time-consuming speeches. This would make Aristotle, as the old saying goes, turn over in his grave.

Examples of the strictly judicial speeches of the courtroom are not, I think, readily found. Today, with press and TV coverage, the public may be informed without hearing the speeches of the judicial opponents (the prosecutor and the defense attorney). The one by Socrates, a famous philosopher, made in his own defense at his trial in Athens still appears in print. Occasionally one runs across the passionate plea Clarence Darrow, a well-known defense lawyer of the 1920s, made to the judge, asking for life imprisonment for his young clients, Leopold and Loeb, rather than death. He was also an advocate for the defense in the Scopes trial (the one where Tennessee accused a young man of teaching the theory of evolution), but we are more likely to remember the speech of the late Spencer Tracy, who played Darrow's part in *Inherit the Wind,* a play and film based on this trial.

There is also the fictitious speech made by Atticus in Harper Lee's *To Kill a Mockingbird.* His defense, although it is the product of the author, does show a recognition of the principles laid down ages earlier.

Even in Supreme Court decisions, the press is more likely to print the opinion of a distinguished justice than the arguments of the advocates in the case.

On the other hand, there is much judicial discourse which goes on outside the courtroom: speeches and articles which judge, accuse or defend a man's decisions, his actions, his conduct. Here the newspapers and TV, sometimes even conversations, acquaint you with the situation and the rhetoric which it calls forth. There is debate and then the vote of censure if the Senate disapproves of a member's conduct. There are the speeches in his defense. Political actions call forth this kind of oratory, so much so that occasionally during our political campaigns the real issues which should govern the voters' decisions are obscured. This kind of judicial speaking is a part of school life as well, for students attack and defend the actions of their classmates and teachers.

*Exercise* 1

*a.* In a way, this exercise is more in the nature of a short play. Divide into groups, each group choosing one member to be the guilty person. Decide what crime he has committed, how it was done, the circumstances surrounding it. Then, instead of writing a brief which would give these details to the court, each crime can be reenacted in class.

*b.* Once the class knows what the defense and prosecutor will be debating, form into groups again and discuss all the things the prosecutor or defense would need to know. What was the motivation for the crime? How has it affected others? Could certain facts have different interpretations? Select your advocates for the defense and for the prosecution and help them plan their speeches to the jury.

*c.* Let the advocates speak, the class serving as jury and deciding, upon the basis of the two speeches, whether the accused is innocent or guilty.

*Note:* No, we haven't yet studied the organization of speeches, but if the discussion was sufficiently lively, the speakers won't have difficulty in presenting their case.

*Exercise 2*

Study the newspaper, or listen to a public affairs program on TV, to see if you can find an example of judicial discourse occurring outside of the courtroom.

### The Deliberative Speech: A Proposal for Future Action

Whether we live in a small town or a city, attend a small school or a big one, we find people take sides. Whether a problem is trivial or important, there will be at least two ways suggested as a solution, and each side tries to persuade the other that its solution is better. This is the occasion for the deliberative speech. It always deals with a current problem but is really concerned with the future, how we shall solve it, if not tomorrow, at some future time.

The speeches or newspaper articles about a new stop light may not be recorded for future generations, but it is rather interesting to poke about in a library and find books containing the deliberative speeches from leaders of the past. The books are usually dusty and unread, for we are more interested in present problems. And it is with today's issues that the beginning writer should be concerned, but a study of these past speeches does show that the writer must be fully committed to his subject.

Educational Television had a program called "The Advocates," patterned, to a certain extent, like a court trial but debating both sides of some issue. The audience was polled at the beginning and end of the program, and it was an example of the power of effective rhetoric to see how the vote changed.

This address was given by Mr. Alfred Gilpin,[1] a member of the Omaha tribe, from Macy, Nebraska, before officials of the Bureau of Indian Affairs, and was concerned with proposed changes in administrative practices. (Since the speech was typed from a tape made at the time, it was possible to note the word or words he particularly stressed. These are in italics.)

What can I say to my Omaha people? That is my main question. For two nights I have stayed awake, looking for honest thoughts and true words to say. I knew my Omaha people would be afraid when they heard

---

[1] Alfred W. Gilpin, Speech made to committee from the Bureau of Indian Affairs (Lincoln, Nebr.: The Nebraska Council for Educational Television, Inc., 1967).

that the Bureau of Indian Affairs was thinking of making a great change in their lives. *It is a poor life, but it is the only one they have to live. The only changes that will not frighten my Omaha people are the changes they make themselves.* These respected officials of the Bureau of Indian Affairs told me my people do not have to be afraid. I stayed awake, trying to know if I could tell them there was nothing to fear. I cannot tell my people that. These honored officials met in Omaha, April 15 and 16, to talk about whether it would be good administration to transfer many services to the county and state, and perhaps to move our Indian Agency away from the Reservation. When I heard that the officials were meeting about such a serious thing, I asked to be allowed to sit with them when they talked. They graciously said I could. I did, for two whole days. The officials said they would consult the people before any changes were made. They are being true to their word. They are consulting, but I have to say this: After the people have been consulted, I am afraid the changes will be made, even if the people do consent to them or not. I think, probably, in Washington, D.C., someone has already decided that the changes will make for a cheaper administration. I think these respected officials are telling my people about how their life is to be changed, not asking whether they want it changed.

I do not think Congress is going to pass a law terminating the Omaha Tribe. I think the Bureau of Indian Affairs is going to terminate the tribe by taking away the Agency services and selling our Omaha lands. I say, most humbly, to the respected officials, that cheaper administration, even better administration, is not *everything*. My poor Omaha people have lived in helplessness for a long time under the Bureau of Indian Affairs. They were taken care of in a way that made them forget to take care of themselves. Today, *they are just waking up . . . just rubbing their eyes . . .* and beginning to hate this helplessness. Today my Omaha people are beginning to fight and to hold what is left of their land, planning how to use the land well. They are beginning to go into County and State politics to protect their American rights. They are beginning to do for themselves the things that the Bureau of Indian Affairs has always done for them. My Omaha people are just beginning to feel *strong and proud,* the way they used to feel before they were made *humble and weak*. Soon they will be able to say to the Bureau of Indian Affairs: *We can take care of ourselves, now. We do not want you.* Why does the Bureau of Indian Affairs pick this moment to say it does not want the Omaha people?

The Omaha Tribal Council has asked the Association on American Indian

Affairs and the University of Nebraska to cooperate in working out a long-range plan for this Omaha community. My people want to see the day when they will not need the special services of the Bureau of Indian Affairs, and this plan will make the day come. I say to these honored officials that any transferral of services, any termination of our Agency, should be part of this long-range plan for the Omaha people, *by* the Omaha people; it should not be planned for them. If the Bureau of Indian Affairs makes big changes in my people's lives, they will remember the lawlessness that came after PL 280 and they will be afraid; they will sink down lower. If my Omaha people are allowed to make their own change, *they will feel brave, proud. They will face the future standing up straight.*

Reviews and tests are all too common in our educational system, so much so that some students may already have been memorizing the answers to these questions:

What is a proposition or thesis statement?

How does a writer appeal to his audience?

What are the special and common topics?

But a child doesn't avoid a hot stove because he has memorized that "a burnt child fears the fire." Probably he touched something which was too hot once and thereafter was careful.

My son's dog didn't learn that he should not go over to the playground because dogs were forbidden there. He learned it by being picked up and taken to the pound. Thereafter he waited at the corner nearest our home.

Therefore, if you really think you understand all that we have been saying about the thesis statement, appeals, and topics, you can show it by your recognition of them in this speech. This is probably better done by class discussion after reading, as not all may agree on some points.

*Exercise 1*

Instead of writing a deliberative speech at this time, let's examine some situations. What is the conflict? Is their any solution? Which side would you be on? Would it be possible for you to get the facts to prove your stand?

Try to think of situations in your own school, your own community. If you can't find any, then consider these.

*a.* The principal of a small high school needs a teacher for two classes in German, but can find no teacher. A citizen in town knows the language and would be willing to help, but he has no teacher-training courses. State law says all teachers must have such courses.

*b.* A new highway will cut through a residential district. The residents complain but are told the state has the plans all drawn and it is too late to change. Besides, it might cost more.

*c.* Miss A takes over Mr. B's job but gets less salary. Miss A is furious.

*d.* A new industrial plant is proposed for the town. It will mean the creation of new jobs; the site will also destroy the town's only decent recreation area.

*Exercise 2*

Magazines like *Look, Life,* and *Time* print letters from readers at the beginning of each issue. You may have skipped them because they are in very small print, sometimes almost obscured by advertisements. These writers express their feelings, for or against some article in a previous issue. Read some of these and try to discover why the writer feels as he does.

CHAPTER NINE

# THE WHOLE COMPOSITION: EACH PART OF THE PLAN FOR THE WHOLE

By now you should be prepared to tackle an entire composition. You have covered words, sentences, and paragraphs and should have some feeling about the part each of these plays in writing.

In addition, you should also be aware (at least I hope you are) that investigation of subject matter concerning an issue has shown you where you stand. For just as Columbus and his sailors could navigate by the North Star only if they knew which was the North Star, so must you know your thesis statement if you are to persuade the reader. And, just as any master workman has his assistants, so do you: the topics, aiding in choice of policy and of arguments; the appeals, ways to secure a desirable reaction from the reader.

Like the architect who has a blueprint for a building, so rhetoric has a plan for composition, showing how the complete work is put together. But in case, despite all I have said before, you have the mistaken idea that the plan is the first step, think once more of the architect. His blueprint is not created immediately. He, too, has to get his thesis, what kind of building it is to be. While he knows much about design, the body of facts about his subject, he may need his particular set of topics to help him choose what he needs for the blueprint: building codes, the climate of the area, kinds of material, the money available, and the building site; whether the building will be for few or many people; any preferences those putting up the money may have. The architect will do many sketches before coming up with his blueprint, his master plan; and the composition student will write everything about his subject, then revise and discard, finally emerging with a composition based upon the plan the rhetoricians of long ago suggested. If the architect's plan is faulty, he won't get the job; if the student's composition is faulty, he can't persuade.

For composition, we have inherited two plans. Aristotle's consists of four parts, but Quintilian, the Roman teacher who seemed more understanding of students' needs, enlarged the four to seven. Here are their plans.

| *Aristotle* | *Quintilian* |
|---|---|
| | 1. Exordium (introduction to win the attention of the audience) |
| 1. Proem (introduction) | 2. Narration (explanation of how the subject came up for discussion) |
| | 3. Exposition (explanation of the point at issue, definition of key terms) |
| 2. Narration (the proposition or thesis statement) | 4. Proposition (explication of the statement to be proved, thesis statement) |
| | 5. Confirmation (arguments for the case to be proved) |
| 3. Argument (body, arguments for the case to be proved) | 6. Refutation (answer to anticipated arguments of the opposition) |
| 4. Epilogue (conclusion) | 7. Peroration (conclusion, summary, final appeal for audience action) |

This plan could be used for the three kinds of composition discussed in the previous chapter: the ceremonial, the judicial, and the deliberative. Since few of us are expected to speak on great occasions or deliver a judicial discourse or formal judgment, the deliberative merits the most attention, for that is the most useful form for daily use. You may ask why other forms of writing are not considered here, but they really go beyond the bounds of the textbook. No doubt the poet, the playwright, and the novelist often seek to persuade, but these authors have qualities no textbook can teach. You can learn to write articles urging conservation, but it takes a John Steinbeck to make us feel the situation in the dust bowl era in his *Grapes of Wrath*.

On the other hand, the plan for the deliberative composition does,

I feel, lend itself to what is called "technical writing," the explanations or summaries written by an employee of some phase of business or industry, at times even a persuasive article urging that a new plan or system be adopted. If you really learn to write the deliberative or persuasive composition, you shouldn't need the "technical writing" course later unless you wish more practice in writing.

But no matter what kind of writing you do, you need a reason or purpose for your plan. The traveler consults a road map with his destination in mind. So, too, must the writer know his destination, that is the particular point of view he wishes his reader to accept, or, as it was called in Chapter Five, the proposition or thesis statement. Then I urged sincere commitment to your subject, but I should also warn you to be objective in presenting the ideas used to prove your proposition, for too much feeling or emotion may fail to convince the reader. There may have been a time when the audience felt sorry for the heroine of the old melodrama. Today this overdose of sentiment draws laughter.

Neither must you obviously suggest that those who disagree with you are incorrect. The bitter and vindictive writer may only antagonize. Think of the reader and his background. You have to understand before you can persuade.

For example, take the subject of dialect. For years our schools have taught that there is one standard way of speaking, that anything else is wrong, and classes drilled and drilled and drilled on usage, none of which, as far as I can tell, had the slightest effect on our speech.

But when I plan to convince teachers that this kind of teaching is useless, that all it does is to frustrate the student and hamper his ability to compose, I can't come right out and say, "You're stupid. This doesn't help."

Instead, I have to work toward an understanding of dialect, to a realization that dialects are added rather than changed, so that the speaker has a choice of language at his disposal. I remind them of the small boy who was talking to his teacher outside of school. When she made some remark to him, he shyly confided, "That isn't the way you'd say it in class." Or to those who feel the lists of the best usage are forever enshrined in the hearts and minds of English teachers, I can point out that many of them say that they are "enthused" about something, whereas every usage section demands "be enthusiastic." I happen to prefer the latter, but if the teacher herself responds to the ordinary usage of the community then certainly the pupils will use the grammatical forms and the vocabulary that they have always heard.

After this, their attitude begins to change. This all takes more time than a stern demand to agree with me, but stern demands rarely persuade those individuals whose ideas are firmly established by tradition.

## A

The old way of beginning a composition was to make an outline, and we have had Roman numerals and capital letters and Arabic numerals and small letters, plus directions that where there is an A there must be a B. But this kind of outline, useful as it is for briefly recording the essential points of a completed piece of work, is only a hindrance when the proposed composition is still only an untidy mass of ideas. Many pupils solved this problem by writing the composition, then the outline, but handing in the outline first as was required, really the only sensible thing to do. Therefore, here are some strategies, or plans, for beginning the composition.

1. *Always* write down your proposition or thesis statement first. This is a great help in knowing what your subject is to be.
2. This second step can be done in several ways.
    *a*. One is to write the composition in your mind; that is, think it over until you really know what you want to write. There is one disadvantage to this method. It does demand a logical mind and the ability to visualize, really to see the sentences in your mind. Frankly, I can't do it.
    *b*. Another way is to write the proposition and then write everything you can possibly say about the subject. This is really a good way to get your ideas down on paper. Naturally, you are going to write again, for this draft will lack organization, may contain irrelevant material, that is, ideas which really don't belong with this subject.
    *c*. A third way is to jot down points you want to make about your subject. I recall a vocational counselor once told us to use this method in choosing a vocation. In one column we were to jot down all our abilities, in the second column all the things we didn't like

to do. For a composition this means jotting down all the points you wish to prove about your subject and then the opponent's view of them. These objections you may want to answer.

## B

Writing the whole composition, therefore, is not writing all the parts and then fitting them together like a jigsaw puzzle. The absence of one part prevents completion of the puzzle; the absence of a part may be quite possible in the composition. If you know your terms are understood as you use them, definition can be omitted. What you do is check your writing to see if you have the material to convince your reader and if you have arranged it in the way best suited to do this.

But just giving directions is rarely enough for learning. If it were, you could drive a car well without practice. Just as you need experience in starting, stopping, and steering a car, you need preliminary practice in writing the parts of a composition.

## C

**The Introduction**

According to Quintilian's plan, three steps come before the thesis statement—the exordium, narration, and definition. These are followed by the thesis statement, and all four can come in an introductory paragraph. You must, however, have the thesis statement in mind before you can write the introductory paragraph.

The *exordium* is really the attention getting sentence. Students seem to like a question as an opener, but while the rhetorical question (one the author answers) is effective later, I doubt if the reader likes to be asked a question before he learns anything about the subject, although it is found as an opener. Probably a writer urging disarmament could begin with "Do you want to be blown up?" and get the reader's attention. On the other hand, the reader might say no to himself and turn to something else.

The *narration* tells why the paper is written, a statement of the facts leading up to the proposition to be argued by the writer. This sentence, for the old kind of assigned topic, could only be "The teacher assigned this." But if you have had any discussion about the topic or thought about it yourself, you can tell why you feel this way and wish to present this point of view.

*Definition,* stating the terms or the parts of the subject to be discussed, is much like the poker player who finds out before he starts what version of the game is being played. In *Presidential Power,* author Richard E. Neustadt[1] knows "presidential" might mean the executive branch of government or the man occupying the office. Therefore, he writes: " 'Presidential' on the title page means nothing but the President. 'Power' means *his* influence. It helps to have these meanings settled at the start."

Last in the paragraph, but foremost in the mind of the author, is the proposition or thesis statement, the subject of the paper.

Here, these four parts for an introduction have been discussed as four sentences, but this means a limited topic. A broader one might mean each sentence was a paragraph; a really broad one would mean not a sentence but a chapter.

For years there have been assignments like a 500- or 1,200-word paper (almost as if numbers had the magic to create a composition) that students find it difficult to believe that length is determined by the breadth of the thesis statement. The old way resulted in adding useless words or subtracting necessary ones, a sure way to turn out poor writing. Students thought of numbers not of ideas.

In the next section (D), discussing the body of the composition, we find this thesis statement: Further space exploration should be discontinued. The following might be the paragraph of introduction.

Men have walked on the moon. (Part 1—This won't get everyone's attention, as no sentence can do that. Many, however, are interested in this achievement.) And while the glory of this technological achievement impressed all people, it has started controversy over its cost. (Part 2—This is the subject brought up for discussion.) For this kind of exploration, discovering not a new continent but another planet, demanding highly trained individuals and the most sophisticated products of technology, is too expensive. (Part 3—General definition for the most part but leading to the thesis statement.) Further space exploration should be discontinued. (Part 4—This is the thesis statement.)

---

[1] Richard E. Neustadt, *Presidential Power* (New York: New American Library, 1964), p. 16.

*The Whole Composition: Each Part of the Plan for the Whole* 103

Together, these four sentences serve as an introduction for the composition discussed in section D.

*Exercise 1*

Try writing the introductory paragraph for a short composition. Remember that the last sentence should be the thesis statement. Although some suggestions follow this, the paragraph will probably be better if you choose your own. But if you have trouble in choosing and in writing, work together with another student. Sometimes, to quote the old saying: "Two heads are better than one."

*a.* Going along with the group is (is not) the best plan.
*b.* My school seemed to encourage (discourage) dropping out.
*c.* Censorship makes a dull film (or book) popular.
*d.* My vote will (will not) make any difference in government.
*e.* Adults in my community stressed the wrong kind of values.
*f.* A technological achievement can cause further problems.
*g.* Retreat from society, like that of Thoreau's, is (is not) a good idea.
*h.* The required course of study often disregards the individual aptitude of the student.

*Exercise 2*

Read the following introductory paragraphs. Discuss how they follow or how they vary from Quintilian's plan for an introduction. Find the thesis statement in each. It may be just suggested.

*a.* In chapter 5 of *Nobody Knows My Name,* James Baldwin begins:

"You can take the child out of the country," my elders were fond of saying, "but you can't take the country out of the child." They were speaking of their own antecedents, I supposed; it didn't, anyway, seem possible that they could be warning me; I took myself out of the country and went to Paris. It was there I discovered that the old folks knew what they were talking about: I found myself, willy-nilly, alchemized into an American the moment I touched French soil.[2]

*b.* Given the current decline of the novel and the parallel decline of poetry and the drama, public interest has turned to the literature of actuality. It may be that in a time of widening uncertainty, and chronic stress the historian's voice is the most needed, the more so as others seem inadequate, often absurd. While the reasons may be argued, the opportunity, I think, is plain for the historian to become the major interpreter in literary experience of man's role

---

[2] James Baldwin, *Nobody Knows My Name* (New York: Dell Publishing Co., 1960), ch. 5, p. 75.

in society. The task is his to provide both the matter to satisfy the public interest and those insights into the human condition without which any reading matter is vapid [dull].[3]

c. In the famous controversy about the two cultures, one important point seems to have been overlooked: that if there truly is a gulf between the literary and the scientific culture, it cannot be bridged by science, but only by language. Language is the only means of communication between specialties as far apart as every individual's unique experience of his own life. Scientific specialization itself is a human experience, and if it is to become part of the general culture it can only be so by communication through language. When there is a question of discussing and explaining our experiences of the other arts, music, or painting, we use words. If architecture aspires to the condition of music, all human experience aspires to words.[4]

d. While four millions of our fellow countrymen are in chains—while men, women, and children are sold on the auction-block with horses, sheep, and swine—while the remorseless slave whip draws the warm blood of our common humanity—it is meet that we assemble as we have done today, and lift up our hearts and voices in earnest denunciation of the vile and shocking abomination. It is not for us to be governed by our hopes or our fears in this great work; yet it is natural on occasions like this, to survey the position of the great struggle which is going on between slavery and freedom, and to dwell upon such signs of encouragement as may have been lately developed, and the state of feeling these signs or events have occasioned in us and among the people generally. It is a fitting time to take an observation—to ascertain [find out] where we are, and what our prospects are.[5]

*Exercise 3*

After almost any meeting people can be seen and heard, standing about and objecting to what was or was not done. If asked why they didn't speak in the meeting, they are likely to answer "I just didn't know how to say what I felt."

The purpose of rhetoric is to enable an individual to say what he feels and to say it effectively, for while we practice written forms, much of our composition is likely to be delivered orally. This takes practice. Effective

---

[3] Barbara W. Tuchman, "The Historian's Opportunity," *The Saturday Review*, February 25, 1967, p. 27.

[4] Stephen Spender, "The Age of Overwrite and Underwrite," *The Saturday Review*, March 12, 1966, p. 21.

[5] Frederick Douglass, "The Dred Scott Decision," in *Great Lives Observed*, edited by Benjamin Quarles (Englewood Cliffs, N.J.: Prentice-Hall, Inc., 1968), p. 59.

*The Whole Composition: Each Part of the Plan for the Whole*   105

action cannot be taken by an individual who passes up his right to speak and just listens to others.

Here are some topics which might be discussed at a meeting. Write the introductory paragraph you might use if you were to talk on one of them. State the topic sentence first. Before any writing is done there should be group discussion with others in your class. This will help you to decide where you stand on this topic. Remember, the thesis statement must be known first.

*Note:* The class may think of topics which concern their area. If so, choose them for discussion.

*a.* Many people competent in vocational work are denied the chance to teach their skills in the public schools because of certain educational requirements for teachers. A group of citizens who feel better vocational training could be obtained if this were not true, discuss the matter with the chairman of the state legislative committee on education.

*b.* A mathematics instructor explains to the board of education why in a beginning mathematics course a study of time payments, loans, etc., is not a waste of time.

*c.* Mrs. X tries to persuade a county political group to support her bid for the office of County Clerk. After all, as she points out, no matter who has held the office, as secretary she has always done the work.

*d.* In an economics class some students argue that unions and management bargain without concern for the general public.

*e.* A college fraternity discusses with a group of alumni why the group put up no decorations for the homecoming game.

*f.* A group of citizens protest the development of a new highway through a residential section.

*g.* A group of women meet with the city council to urge that there be more centers for voter registration.

# D

### The Body of the Composition

Quintilian divided the body of the composition into two parts: *confirmation,* points to prove the thesis statement; *refutation,* the answering of objections to the subject. Telling a student just how many points to make, just how to arrange them is really not possible. His choices depend upon the situation.

Perhaps we should recognize that one or two points, well-explained, with good examples for each, are more effective than more points hastily presented. Then, too, we should recognize that answering an opponent's objections makes our argument more persuasive.

At the present time there is discussion, now that we have reached the moon, of more space exploration, even of going on to Mars. Perhaps you haven't really considered this, aren't really sure where you stand. Thus, you read, you talk to others, you listen, for it is helpful to talk about your subject with other students. Composition—and while this sounds as if I am off the subject, I am not—has sometimes been considered as a skill apart from language. It simply is not true. Ideas cannot be put on paper until they are words in the mind. This is why I regret that subjects for composition are rarely a part of student conversation. Over a coke one can talk and discuss, thus putting what was a cloudy picture into focus. This is not plagiarism or copying. If authors did not observe and talk, there would be much less writing. And out of such discussion can come a variety of points to jot down on paper.

1. Space exploration is too expensive.
2. We need to solve problems on earth first.
3. There are scientific discoveries which are good.
4. Mechanical methods can be used to bring back rocks. Men are not needed. This will cut expenses.
5. Such scientific technology should be applied to problems like air and water pollution.
6. Success in space exploration adds to the prestige of our country.
7. The trip to the moon brought the peoples of the world together in their interest.
8. Young people need heroes, like the astronauts.
9. Even if money isn't spent on space exploration, Congress will never appropriate it for our problems here on earth.
10. This would solve our population problem.

At this point you have to make up your mind. Do you or don't you approve of further exploration in space?

Let's assume you choose this thesis statement:

> Further space exploration should be discontinued.

But a thesis statement is not a composition and the points drawn from

# The Whole Composition: Each Part of the Plan for the Whole

discussion may not be enough. It is time to use the topics mentioned in Chapter Seven. Definition was the first, and while you know how to define this you probably feel that your reader also understands. You are also confident that you and your reader understand the problem of pollution, although, as you think this over, you decide that specific description of some form of pollution might be worthwhile.

Comparison may be a puzzle until you begin to recall past explorations. Surely the discovery of America was exciting to past ages. This could be used in arguing that space exploration should be continued and yet you want to prove that it should cease. But the thought of this discovery brings to mind the story of Spain, its presence in the New World and the decline which followed. You remember the quarrels between European countries over the New World territory. Would nations begin to fight about space?

Without realizing it, perhaps, comparison has led to relationship so you go further. The smoggy sky above shows what technology has done to your environment and you begin to wonder if space exploration will pollute the universe. Where, you think, do all those objects go that the astronauts discard before they return? Are they all burned up or is that debris still floating around? And you ask yourself if all this money should not be spent to bring back clear streams and a blue sky.

The cars whiz by, polluting the air and causing traffic jams, proving that discoveries don't always solve problems. You may remember reading that breathing the air filled with the fumes of a car's exhaust can cause lung cancer. Would something like this soon happen if space were populated?

Or there is the topic of circumstance. Would the money saved really be used for worthwhile projects? Your reader may be cynical about the actions of Congress and yet there was the TVA, the National Parks, and the Land Grant Colleges.

As to testimony, you find you can't recall exact figures about the cost of space exploration. Yet you know you have seen or heard them. Perhaps going to the library and consulting the *Reader's Guide* would help here.

Thus you have points in mind. But what of the special topics? Both could really be applied, but after mulling this all over in your mind, you would probably decide that your approach should deal mainly with that of expediency, although with overtones of the good as you do imply worthy uses for the money saved.

At this point your plan for the composition might be more like that of this chart.

### THE CHART FOR THE SPECIAL TOPICS

| The Worthy or Good | The Expedient or Useful |
|---|---|
|  | 1. Space exploration is too expensive. |
| 2. We need to solve problems on earth first. |  |
| 5. Such scientific technology should be applied to problems like air and water pollution. |  |
| 6. Success in space exploration adds to the prestige of our country. |  |
| 7. The trip to the moon brought the peoples of the world together in their interest. |  |
|  | 9. Even if money isn't spent on space exploration, Congress will never appropriate it for our problems here on earth. |
| 10. This would solve our population problem. |  |

Notice that this plan omits the original points 3, 4, and 8. Your reason for doing so may not have been this definite, but this reasoning probably took place, in your mind if not on paper.

The term "scientific discoveries" is too broad. It could be space exploration, the polio vaccine, the TV. Your proposition calls for total elimination of funds and point 4 suggests just cutting down. You and the reader both accept the need for heroes, yet the astronauts were not

## The Whole Composition: Each Part of the Plan for the Whole 109

the only ones responsible for successful space flights. They were just the visible ones.

Points 2, 5, and 10 are practical aims, yet as they add to the quality of life they are like the special topic of the good. Perhaps you decide to emphasize this second one.

As you think of points 6, 7, and 10 you realize that these are arguments for those who want to go on, say to Mars. They need to be refuted, while points 1, 2, 5, and 9 can serve as confirmation, definite points for persuasion.

All of this probably sounds, as I should undoubtedly say if you were in my class, like a hell of a lot of work. But a step-by-step description of a process usually does seem laborious. The diagrams and directions for putting together a simple bookcase seemed complicated until I began to work with the parts. (And don't be discouraged if you have trouble early in the project. On my first attempt, the bookcase collapsed.)

For you are ready by now to begin writing the body of the composition. The knowledge the topics recalled should make you more confident of proving each point of the argument, and as you write, other examples may come to mind. Remember your decision to write of the problems caused by the automobile? Add the stories of the older relative who tells of the fun he had driving his old Model A and compare it with a description of today's driving. It will make your reader add even more. He drives too.

You may have felt that expansion by the use of myths or fables was just an exercise, but one could be used here. Pride in space exploration, particularly when it causes people to neglect needed improvements on their own planet, comes close to the wilful pride of Phaethon, whose sun chariot seared the earth.

Once you start writing (and making yourself sit down to it is really the hardest part) you can get several pages quite readily. Then, if you really want to persuade, you revise for order and for more effective words and sentences.

*Exercise* 1

Try expanding one of the following points of this composition.

*a.* Choosing point 1 as your topic sentence, explain it in terms of managing your own budget. Or you could use the story of the ant and the grasshopper. The grasshopper, you recall, made no preparation for the future.

*b.* Choosing point 2 as your topic sentence, expand it into a paragraph, using an example of air or water pollution in your own community.

*c.* Choosing point 6 as your topic sentence, you might use the old saying "Pride goeth before a fall" as proof, with an extra example from your own observation of life.

# E

### Conclusion or Peroration

Our old texts discussed this paragraph as a summary of points made in the body of the theme, but this does tend to be dull. Cicero, the Roman orator, suggested emphasizing the strongest point again. Usually we find that the author who is really persuasive puts his emotional appeal in this part. He may begin by generalizing, then emphasize his strongest point, appeal to the emotions of his reader, then end with a thesis statement, although not in the terms of the original one. There will be, of course, variations of this.

Suppose we consider a concluding paragraph for our composition about further space exploration. We might say:

> In conclusion, I can only believe that further space exploration will do little to improve life on this earth.

After this we could add once again a sentence or so concerning the expenditures necessary. But people react to fear as well as to thrift; therefore we could follow with a picture of an earth which DDT and waste have made uninhabitable, or will unless we do something about it. People also react to ideas of hope, of imagination, so we could add that the charm of the moon has been lost, that now it is no longer a lovely silver crescent in the sky but a picture in our mind of a flat desert with craters. We could remind the reader that man needs dreams and refer to the hunter's moon of the Indians, the silvery moon of the Greek goddess Diana. And finally, our thesis statement again, but put it into different words.

*Exercise 1*

By this time you may feel that you really have written a composition on discontinuing space exploration. Therefore, you probably can write a concluding paragraph, following the suggestions given for the conclusion.

## F

To you this case of *The Poor Man's Bees* may seem trivial, but it had certain merits for students of the past. The case emphasized the principle that a poor man should not suffer because of the whims of the rich, and suffering would follow the loss of bees since honey was a staple in his diet. Although what follows is the outline of the case the poor man represented (he would speak for himself in the society of that time), he might have gone to the professional rhetorician for assistance, and Quintilian was expecting some of his students to become such professionals. There is even a modern touch in his direction for "impersonation," to speak as the poor man would have done. Today the term is role-playing. Even the narration has an appeal that is still acceptable, the simple country life, a kind of existence that the present commune may be seeking. In the peroration, there is less really of a praise of bees than of the virtues we still admire: order, industry, loyalty.

But instead of developing the case Quintilian outlines, study it, and then do one of the following exercises.

### *The Poor Man's Bees*[6]

One of the most famous as well as one of the most charming of the Roman . . . [judicial cases] bears the traditional title *The Poor Man's Bees*. It is the thirteenth of the major declamations of Quintilian. The theme is this: "The law allows an action for injuries suffered wrongfully . . . . A poor man and a rich man were neighbors in the country; their gardens joined. The rich man had flowers in his garden; the poor man, bees. The rich man complained that his flowers were injured by the poor man's bees. He demanded that the bees be removed. When the poor man failed to remove them, the rich man sprinkled poison on his flowers. The poor man's bees all died of the poison. He brings action against the rich man for injuries suffered wrongfully."

This . . . [case] turns entirely on the status of quality. The facts are admitted by both sides. The rich man did poison the poor man's bees. The poor man did suffer damage. But was the damage suffered wrongfully? The whole speech, . . . [an impersonation] spoken as by the poor man, has no

---

[6] Donald Leman Clark, *Rhetoric in Greco-Roman Education* (New York: Columbia University Press, 1963), pp. 247–50.

other end than to dilate on the essential wrongness of the rich man and his bee poisoning and the essential rightness of the poor man and his bees. I subjoin a summary outline of the poor man's plea.

*Exordium.* It may seem strange that I, a poor man, should have the daring to sue a rich and powerful enemy, but now my bees are killed, I have nothing to live for. This may seem an insignificant case, but to me, a poor man, the bees were all I had.

*Narration.* The rich man has built up a large estate by buying up small holdings. Only my small holding remains, completely surrounded by his estate. [This is colored by a long . . . (detailed account) on the little farm and the simple and pure pleasures of a frugal country life. This is followed by a . . . (imitation of the way the poor man spoke) dramatically presenting the rich man in the act of arrogantly ordering the bees removed. Then . . . (a detailed account), to arouse sympathy, on how the bees suffered and died as a result of the poison.]

*Confirmation.* It is illegal for anyone to possess poison. Possession of poison is evidence of malicious intent. He might as well have poisoned a man as the bees. Enemies are easier to find than poison. A poor man is at a disadvantage when a rich man attacks him. If I got more bees, he might poison them.

*Status.* He admits the fact that he poisoned my bees . . . . The question in his plea is, Was damage done . . . and if so, Was it done wrongfully . . . ?

*Refutation.*
(1) He claims it was not a damage because bees are wild.
(2) He claims it was not done wrongfully, because
    (a) he did it on his own land;
    (b) the bees had damaged his flowers;
    (c) he used only a little poison;
    (d) the bees came of their own accord.
(1') But it was a damage, because
    (a) it is a damage to lose what it is an advantage to keep;
    (b) the bees were not wild but a homebred swarm;
    (c) all domestic animals were once wild and slaves were once free;
    (d) the bees were my property and my main source of income.
(2') Moreover the damage was done wrongfully, because
    (a) if he killed a man on his own land, he would be guilty of murder; hence by killing my bees on his own land he is guilty of wrongful damage.

(b) if my bees did damage to the flowers in his garden, he should have sued me for damages instead of taking the law into his own hands. If the loss of a few flowers be such a damage to a rich man, how much greater the loss of all my bees to me. [Here follows . . . (a detailed description) on how little damage bees do to flowers and how quickly flowers fade.] He is ungrateful because I used to give him honey every year. [Further dilation on the rich man's wealth and power and the poor man's poverty and weakness.]

(c) [The small amount of poison is not mentioned in the refutation.]

(d) That the bees came to the poison of their own accord is no defense, because a man might walk into an ambush of his own accord. What was the rich man's intention? That he destroy my bees. What was the result? That he did destroy them. I suffer a personal loss as well as a property loss because I was fond of my bees.

*Peroration or Conclusion*

[. . . (A speech in praise) of bees]

(1) Bees do not take offense when we take their honey.
(2) Other domestic animals have to be trained and controlled, but bees work without our bidding.
(3) Other animals injure crops, but not bees.
(4) Men find poison; bees, honey.

. . . . .

(7) Men have to learn mechanical arts, but bees are natural-born mechanics.
(8) A bee hive is a model of civil polity, for
    (a) the life of bees is ordered;
    (b) they save against the future;
    (c) they work for the common good;
    (d) they are industrious;
    (e) they are loyal.
(9) Their combs are works of art.
(10) Their honey is useful as
    (a) medicine;
    (b) food.

Hence, one who would poison bees is unnaturally cruel. The irony is that the man who put poison on his flowers to poison my bees killed his own flowers with the poison.

*Exercise 1*

According to newspaper accounts a citizen waged his own battle against the company which polluted his favorite fishing stream: first by blocking a waste pipe, forcing the filthy waste back into the plant; later by invading the company offices and dumping a container of the foul-smelling liquid from the polluted stream upon the floor. But in his case, he will eventually be caught and sued for property damage. Since those laws are more firmly established than laws against pollution, he is likely to be convicted. His attorney can argue, in extenuation of his actions, that only when made personally aware of the results of pollution are the company officials likely to act; he can suggest that his client desires to save the countryside. The peroration can hardly use fish, as Quintilian did the bees, as representatives of order, industry, and loyalty, but can present the idea that men can perfect themselves by close contact with the beauty of nature and that his client's actions show a desire to make this possible.

If you stop to think about it, however, the rhetoric in Quintilian's case is being used to establish a principle more concerned with justice, for you could hardly expect the poor man's bees to neglect flowers. In the modern case, the aims of the citizen may be laudable, but he really accomplishes little. His actions become an amusing escapade for the reporters, a nuisance for the company.

But suppose, instead, he began a campaign against the company, appearing before a town council or state legislature to ask for more stringent laws on pollution or enforcement of those already passed. The argument could be much the same as that already discussed, but here you don't have to defend a precarious case and you can argue about a humanitarian principle. Work out the case which could be presented. Dividing into groups and pooling the results of group discussion will probably make this easier.

*Exercise 2*

Although companies support the idea of eradicating pollution, they will often argue against particularly stringent measures. Even the people may support such industrial development if it means jobs. Try creating a case for this side of the debate on pollution.

CHAPTER TEN

# THE ENTIRE COMPOSITION: JOINING ALL THE PARTS TOGETHER

In case you feel that it has taken forever to reach the stage of writing more than bits and pieces, remember the old saying: Rome wasn't built in a day. Remember as well that while later life outside the classroom may not demand much writing, this practice should enable you, when necessary, to express your ideas orally. This study of rhetoric should do more. It should prevent your being taken in by the false rhetoric which bombards us.

As is, no doubt, apparent, I feel that we need to do more about problems in our country. Thus, if someone talks or writes about continuing space exploration in terms of the glorious days of the past when we conquered the West or says that if we do not continue we shall "lose face," I shall think he is evading the issue. If he wants to convince me, he has to make real points, practical ones. But if I were ignorant of the true art of persuasion, he might convince me. Whether you read or listen, think.

This speech was made by the late President Kennedy, then a Senator, in the campaign of 1960. While we have never as a nation let our religious differences lead us to a civil war, yet religious tolerance has not always been practiced. Even the Puritans who came seeking religious freedom expelled Roger Williams, the Quaker, from their colony.

Although Catholics held offices in our political structure, no Catholic had ever been elected as president. When Al Smith ran, the issue of Catholicism was clouded by his support for the repeal of prohibition. When Kennedy ran, the issue was clearly one of religion. Instead of hedging, he preferred to meet the issue squarely and made, as the introductory note explains, the following speech.[1]

## John Fitzgerald Kennedy, 1917–1963

This speech was made by Senator Kennedy to the Greater Houston (Texas) Ministerial Association on September 12, 1960. As the Democratic nominee for the presidency, Kennedy was obliged to confront much strong feelings against a Catholic becoming President. The remarks here are the result of his effort to combine with dignity a statement of personal belief with a political purpose.

### Religion in Government

I am grateful for your generous invitation to state my views.

While the so-called religious issue is necessarily and properly the chief topic here tonight, I want to emphasize from the outset that I believe that we have far more critical issues in the 1960 election: the spread of Communist influence, until it now festers only ninety miles off the coast of Florida—the humiliating treatment of our President and Vice President by those who no longer respect our power—the hungry children I saw in West Virginia, the old people who cannot pay their doctor's bills, the families forced to give up their farms—an America with too many slums, with too few schools, and too late to the moon and outer space.

These are the real issues which should decide this campaign. And they are not religious issues—for war and hunger and ignorance and despair know no religious barrier.

But because I am a Catholic, and no Catholic has ever been elected President, the real issues in this campaign have been obscured—perhaps deliberately in some quarters less responsible than this. So it is apparently necessary for me to state once again—not what kind of church I believe in, for that should be important only to me, but what kind of America I believe in.

I believe in an America where the separation of church and state is absolute—where no Catholic prelate would tell the President (should he be a Catholic) how to act and no Protestant minister would tell his parishioners for whom to vote—where no church or church school is

---

[1] George W. Hibbitt, ed., *The Dolphin Book of Speeches* (Garden City, N.Y.: Doubleday & Co., Inc., 1965), pp. 178–82.

granted any public funds or political preference—and where no man is denied public office merely because his religion differs from the President who might appoint him or the people who might elect him.

I believe in an America that is officially neither Catholic, Protestant nor Jewish—where no public official either requests or accepts instructions on public policy from the Pope, the National Council of Churches or any other ecclesiastical source—where no religious body seeks to impose its will directly or indirectly upon the general populace or the public acts of its officials—and where religious liberty is so indivisible that an act against one church is treated as an act against all.

For while this year it may be a Catholic against whom the finger of suspicion is pointed, in other years it has been, or may someday be again, a Jew—or a Quaker—or a Unitarian—or a Baptist. It was Virginia's harassment of Baptist preachers, for example, that led to Jefferson's statute of religious freedom. Today, I may be the victim—but tomorrow it may be you—until the whole fabric of our harmonious society is ripped apart at a time of great national peril.

Finally, I believe in an America where religious intolerance will someday end—where all men and all churches are treated as equal—where every man has the same right to attend or not attend the church of his choice—where there is no Catholic vote, no anti-Catholic vote, no bloc voting of any kind—and where Catholics, Protestants and Jews, both the lay and the pastoral level, will refrain from those attitudes of disdain and division which have so often marred their works in the past, and promote instead the American ideal of brotherhood.

That is the kind of America in which I believe. And it represents the kind of Presidency in which I believe—a great office that must be neither humbled by making it the instrument of any religious group, nor tarnished by arbitrarily withholding it, its occupancy, from the member of any religious group. I believe in a President whose views on religion are his own private affair, neither imposed upon him by the nation or imposed by the nation upon him as a condition to holding that office.

I would not look with favor upon a President working to subvert the First Amendment's guarantees of religious liberty (nor would our system of checks and balances permit him to do so). And neither do I look with favor upon those who would work to subvert Article VI of the Constitution by requiring a religious test—even by indirection—for if they disagree with that safeguard, they should be openly working to repeal it.

I want a Chief Executive whose public acts are responsible to all and obligated to none—who can attend any ceremony, service or dinner his office may appropriately require him to fulfill—and whose fulfillment of his Presidential office is not limited or conditioned by any religious oath, ritual or obligation.

This is the kind of America I believe in—and this is the kind of America I fought for in the South Pacific and the kind my brother died for in Europe. No one suggested then that we might have a "divided loyalty," that we did "not believe in liberty" or that we belonged to a disloyal group that threatened "the freedom for which our forefathers died."

And in fact this is the kind of America for which our forefathers did die when they fled here to escape religious test oaths, that denied office to members of less favored churches, when they fought for the Constitution, the Bill of Rights, the Virginia Statute of Religious Freedom—and when they fought at the shrine I visited today—the Alamo. For side by side with Bowie and Crockett died Fuentes and McCafferty and Bailey and Bedillo and Carey—but no one knows whether they were Catholics or not. For there was no religious test there.

I ask you tonight to follow in that tradition, to judge me on the basis of fourteen years in the Congress—on my declared stands against an ambassador to the Vatican, against unconstitutional aid to parochial schools, and against any boycott of the public schools (which I attended myself)—instead of judging me on the basis of these pamphlets and publications we have all seen that carefully select quotations out of context from the statements of Catholic Church leaders, usually in other countries, frequently in other centuries, and rarely relevant to any situation here—and always omitting, of course, that statement of the American bishops in 1948 which strongly endorsed church-state separation.

I do not consider these other quotations binding upon my public acts—why should you? But let me say, with respect to other countries, that I am wholly opposed to the state being used by any religious group, Catholic or Protestant, to compel, prohibit or persecute the free exercise of any other religion. And that goes for any persecution at any time, by anyone, in any country.

And I hope that you and I condemn with equal fervor those nations which deny their Presidency to Protestants and those which deny it to Catholics. And rather than cite the misdeeds of those who differ, I would also cite the record of the Catholic Church in such nations as France and

Ireland—and the independence of such statesmen as de Gaulle and Adenauer.

But let me stress again that these are my views—for contrary to common newspaper usage, I am not the Catholic candidate for President. I am the Democratic Party's candidate for President, who happens also to be a Catholic.

I do not speak for my church on public matters—and the church does not speak for me.

Whatever issue may come before me as President, if I should be elected—on birth control, divorce, censorship, gambling, or any other subject—I will make my decision in accordance with these views, in accordance with what my conscience tells me to be in the national interest, and without regard to outside religious pressure or dictate. And no power or threat of punishment could cause me to decide otherwise.

But if the time should ever come—and I do not concede any conflict to be remotely possible—when my office would require me to either violate my conscience, or violate the national interest, then I would resign the office, and I hope any other conscientious public servant would do likewise.

But I do not intend to apologize for these views to my critics of either Catholic or Protestant faith, nor do I intend to disavow either my views or my church in order to win this election. If I should lose on the real issues, I shall return to my seat in the Senate, satisfied that I tried my best and was fairly judged.

But if this election is decided on the basis that forty million Americans lost their chance of being President on the day they were baptized, then it is the whole nation that will be the loser in the eyes of Catholics and non-Catholics around the world, in the eyes of history, and in the eyes of our own people.

But if, on the other hand, I should win the election, I shall devote every effort of mind and spirit to fulfilling the oath of the Presidency—practically identical, I might add, with the oath I have taken for fourteen years in the Congress. For, without reservation, I can, and I quote, "solemnly swear that I will faithfully execute the office of President of the United States and will to the best of my ability preserve, protect and defend the Constitution, so help me God."

*Exercise 1*

*a.* How does Kennedy establish his ethos? Remember that, in general, he was speaking to a group opposed to him.

*b.* What is his thesis statement? Have you been introduced to it earlier in this text?

*c.* What points does he make to prove this thesis?

*d.* How does he reveal his understanding of the objections this group has? In what way would such understanding strengthen his appeal?

*e.* Why does he emphasize the kind of president this country needs?

*f.* Why does he not recount, as he so easily could have done, the previous struggles of the Catholic immigrant to this country?

*g.* Does his frequent use of "I believe in" strengthen or weaken the discourse?

*h.* Why does he refer to the battle of the Alamo instead of a battle of our Civil War?

*i.* For what reason does he refer, in the next to the last paragraph, to this election as seen from an international point of view?

*j.* Is there any evidence you can find of any kind of emotional appeal to his audience?

*Exercise 2*

At this point, I wish we had schools of rhetoric, for just as the judoka can go to a gym and find an opponent for a practice match, so could the rhetorical student of ancient days join a group engaging in arguments in which he joined, carrying this practice on debate of problems over into his later life as a citizen.

For to speak or write well on a subject one must be involved with it. Perhaps our educational system itself has been at fault, teachers telling students that Shakespeare is a great writer instead of letting students discover that even in Shakespeare's time many of today's problems existed, problems our student finds, problems with which he is involved.

Therefore, I hesitate to do, as textbooks have often done, assign a topic to you. But here is an essay urging a new kind of university. And since this matter of college education is one that does involve many students, you should be able to decide whether you are for or against John Fischer's suggested university.

Write a composition urging acceptance of this plan or one in which you oppose it, but discuss it all in class first. Small groups are best for this.

## The Entire Composition: Joining All the Parts Together

### *The Easy Chair*[2]

Survival U: Prospectus for a Really
Relevant University

"It gets pretty depressing to watch what is going on in the world and realize that your education is not equipping you to do anything about it."

—From a letter by a University of California senior

She is not a radical, and has never taken part in any demonstration. She will graduate with honors, and profound disillusionment. From listening to her—and a good many like-minded students at California and East Coast campuses—I think I am beginning to understand what they mean when they say that a liberal-arts education isn't relevant.

They mean it is incoherent. It doesn't cohere. It consists of bits and pieces which don't stick together, and have no common purpose. One of our leading Negro educators, Arthur Lewis of Princeton, recently summed it up better than I can. America is the only country, he said, where youngsters are required "to fritter away their precious years in meaningless peregrination from subject to subject . . . spending twelve weeks getting some tidbits of religion, twelve weeks learning French, twelve weeks seeing whether the history professor is stimulating, twelve weeks seeking entertainment from the economics professor, twelve weeks confirming that one is not going to be able to master calculus."

These fragments are meaningless because they are not organized around any central purpose, or vision of the world. The typical liberal-arts college has no clearly defined goals. It merely offers a smorgasbord of courses, in hopes that if a student nibbles at a few dishes from the humanities table, plus a snack of science, and a garnish of art or anthropology, he may emerge as "a cultivated man"—whatever that means. Except for a few surviving church schools, no university even pretends to have a unifying philosophy. Individual teachers may have personal ideologies—but since they are likely to range, on any given campus, from Marxism to worship of the scientific method to exaltation of the irrational (*a la* Norman O. Brown), they don't cohere either. They often leave a student convinced at the end of four years that any given idea is probably about as valid as any other—and that none of them has much relationship to the others, or to the decisions he is going to have to make the day after graduation.

Education was not always like that. The earliest European universities had a precise purpose: to train an elite for the service of the Church. Everything they taught was focused to that end. Thomas Aquinas had spelled it all out: what

---

[2] John Fischer, "The Easy Chair," *Harper's,* September, 1969, pp. 12, 14, 17, 20, 22.

subjects had to be mastered, how each connected with every other, and what meaning they had for man and God.

Later, for a span of several centuries, Oxford and Cambridge had an equally clear function: to train administrators to run an empire. So too did Harvard and Yale at the time they were founded; their job was to produce the clergymen, lawyers, and doctors that a new country needed. In each case, the curriculum was rigidly prescribed. A student learned what he needed, to prepare himself to be a competent priest, district officer, or surgeon. He had no doubts about the relevance of his courses—and no time to fret about expanding his consciousness or currying his sensual awareness.

This is still true of our professional schools. I have yet to hear an engineering or medical student complain that his education is meaningless. Only in the liberal-arts colleges—which boast that "we are not trade schools"—do the youngsters get that feeling that they are drowning in a cloud of feathers.

For a long while some of our less complacent academics have been trying to restore coherence to American education. When Robert Hutchins was at Chicago, he tried to use the Great Books to build a comprehensible framework for the main ideas of civilized man. His experiment is still being carried on, with some modifications, at St. John's—but it has not proved irresistibly contagious. Sure, the thoughts of Plato and Machiavelli are still pertinent, so far as they go—but somehow they don't seem quite enough armor for a world beset with splitting atoms, urban guerrillas, nineteen varieties of psychotherapists, amplified guitars, napalm, computers, astronauts, and an atmosphere polluted simultaneously with auto exhaust and TV commercials.

Another strategy for linking together the bits-and-pieces has been attempted at Harvard and at a number of other universities. They require their students to take at least two years of survey courses, known variously as core studies, general education, or world civilization. These too have been something less than triumphantly successful. Most faculty members don't like to teach them, regarding them as superficial and synthetic. (And right they are, since no survey course that I know of has a strong unifying concept to give it focus.) Moreover, the senior professors shun such courses in favor of their own narrow specialities. Consequently, the core studies which are meant to place all human experience—well, at least the brightest nuggets—into One Big Picture usually end up in the perfunctory hands of resentful junior teachers. Naturally the undergraduates don't take them seriously either.

Any successful reform of American education, I am now convinced, will have to be far more revolutionary than anything yet attempted. At a minimum, it should be:

1. Founded on a single guiding concept—an idea capable of knotting together all strands of study, thus giving them both coherence and visible purpose.

2. Capable of equipping young people to do something about "what is going on in the world"—notably the things which bother them most, including war, injustice, racial conflict, and the quality of life.

Maybe it isn't possible. Perhaps knowledge is proliferating so fast, and in so many directions, that it can never again be ordered into a coherent whole, so that molecular biology, Robert Lowell's poetry, and highway engineering will seem relevant to each other and to the lives of ordinary people. Quite possibly the knowledge explosion, as Peter F. Drucker has called it, dooms us to scholarship which grows steadily more specialized, fragmented, and incomprehensible.

The Soviet experience is hardly encouraging. Russian education is built on what is meant to be a unifying ideology: Marxism-Leninism. In theory, it provides an organizing principle for all scholarly activity—whether history, literature, genetics, or military science. Its purpose is explicit: to train a Communist elite for the greater power and glory of the Soviet state, just as the medieval universities trained a priesthood to serve the Church.

Yet according to all accounts that I have seen, it doesn't work very well. Soviet intellectuals apparently are almost as restless and unhappy as our own. Increasing numbers of them are finding Marxism-Leninism too simplistic, too narrowly doctrinaire, too oppressive; the bravest are risking prison in order to pursue their own heretical visions of reality.

Is it conceivable, then, that we might hit upon another idea which could serve as the organizing principle for many fields of scholarly inquiry; which is relevant to the urgent needs of our time; and which would not, on the other hand, impose an ideological strait jacket, as both ecclesiastical and Marxist education attempted to do?

Just possibly it could be done. For the last two or three years I have been probing around among professors, college administrators, and students—and so far I have come up with only one idea which might fit the specifications. It is simply the idea of survival.

For the first time in history, the future of the human race is now in serious question. This fact is hard to believe, or even think about—yet it is the message which a growing number of scientists are trying, almost frantically, to get across to us. Listen, for example, to Professor Richard A. Falk of Princeton and of the Center for Advanced Study in the Behavioral Sciences:

"The planet and mankind are in grave danger of irreversible catastrophe . . . Man may be skeptical about following the flight of the dodo into extinction, but the evidence points increasingly to just such a pursuit. . . . There are four interconnected threats to the planet—wars of mass destruction, overpopulation, pollution, and the depletion of resources. They have a cumulative effect. A problem in one area renders it more difficult to solve the problems in any other area. . . . The basis of all four problems is the inadequacy of the sovereign states to manage the affairs of mankind in the twentieth century."

Similar warnings could be quoted from a long list of other social scientists, biologists, and physicists, among them such distinguished thinkers as Rene Dubos, Buckminster Fuller, Loren Eiseley, George Wald, and Barry Commoner. They are not hopeless. Most of them believe that we still have a chance to bring our weapons, our population growth, and the destruction of our environment under control before it is too late. But the time is short, and so far there is no evidence that enough people are taking them seriously.

That would be the prime aim of the experimental university I'm suggesting here: to look seriously at the interlinking threats to human existence, and to learn what we can do to fight them off.

Let's call it Survival U. It will not be a multiversity, offering courses in every conceivable field. Its motto—emblazoned on a life jacket rampant—will be: "What must we do to be saved?" If a course does not help to answer that question, it will not be taught here. Students interested in musicology, junk sculpture, the Theater of the Absurd, and the literary *dicta* of Leslie Fiedler can go somewhere else.

Neither will our professors be detached, dispassionate scholars. To get hired, each will have to demonstrate an emotional commitment to our cause. Moreover, he will be expected to be a moralist; for this generation of students, like no other in my lifetime, is hungering and thirsting after righteousness. What it wants is a moral system it can believe in—and that is what our university will try to provide. In every class it will preach the primordial ethic of survival.

The biology department, for example, will point out that it is sinful for anybody to have more than two children. It has long since become glaringly evident that unless the earth's cancerous growth of population can be halted, all other problems—poverty, war, racial strife, uninhabitable cities, and the rest—are beyond solution. So the department naturally will teach all known methods of birth control, and much of its research will be aimed at perfecting cheaper and better ones.

Its second lesson in biological morality will be: "Nobody has a right to poison the environment we live in." This maxim will be illustrated by a list of public enemies. At the top will stand the politicians, scientists, and military men—of whatever country—who make and deploy atomic weapons; for if these are ever used, even in so-called defensive systems like the ABM, the atmosphere will be so contaminated with strontium 90 and other radioactive

## The Entire Composition: Joining All the Parts Together 125

isotopes that human survival seems most unlikely. Also on the list will be anybody who makes or tests chemical and biological weapons—or who even attempts to get rid of obsolete nerve gas, as our Army recently proposed, by dumping the stuff in the sea.

Only slightly less wicked, our biology profs will indicate, is the farmer who drenches his land with DDT. Such insecticides remain virulent indefinitely, and as they wash into the streams and oceans they poison fish, water fowl, and eventually the people who eat them. Worse yet—as John Hay noted in his recently published *In Defense of Nature*—"The original small, diluted concentrations of these chemicals tend to build up in a food chain so as to end in a concentration that may be thousands of times as strong." It is rapidly spreading throughout the globe. DDT already has been found in the tissues of Eskimos and of Antarctic penguins, so it seems probable that similar deposits are gradually building up in your body and mine. The minimum fatal dosage is still unknown.

Before he finishes this course, a student may begin to feel twinges of conscience himself. Is his motorcycle exhaust adding carbon monoxide to the smog we breathe? Is his sewage polluting the nearest river? If so, he will be reminded of two proverbs. From Jesus: "Let him who is without sin among you cast the first stone." From Pogo: "We have met the enemy and he is us."

In like fashion, our engineering students will learn not only how to build dams and highways, but where *not* to build them. Unless they understand that it is immoral to flood the Grand Canyon or destroy the Everglades with a jetport, they will never pass the final exam. Indeed, our engineering graduates will be trained to ask a key question about every contract offered them: "What will be its effect on human life?" That obviously will lead to other questions which every engineer ought to comprehend as thoroughly as his slide rule. Is this new highway really necessary? Would it be wiser to use the money for mass transit—or to decongest traffic by building a new city somewhere else? Is an offshore oil well really a good idea, in view of what happened to Santa Barbara?

Our engineering faculty also will specialize in training men for a new growth industry: garbage disposal. Americans already are spending $4.5 billion a year to collect and get rid of the garbage which we produce more profusely than any other people (more than five pounds a day for each of us). But unless we are resigned to stifling in our own trash, we are going to have to come up with at least an additional $835 million a year.[3] Any industry with a growth rate of 18 per cent offers obvious attractions to a bright young man—and

---

[3] According to Richard D. Vaughn, chief of the Solid Wastes Program of HEW, in his recent horror story entitled "1968 Survey of Community Solid Waste Practices."

if he can figure out a new way to get rid of our offal, his fortune will be unlimited.

Because the old ways no longer work. Every big city in the United States is running out of dumping grounds. Burning won't do either, since the air is dangerously polluted already—and in any case, 75 per cent of the incinerators in use are inadequate. For some 150 years Californians happily piled their garbage into San Francisco Bay, but they can't much longer. Dump-and-fill operations already have reduced it to half its original size, and in a few more decades it would be possible to walk dry-shod from Oakland to the Embarcadero. Consequently San Francisco is now planning to ship garbage 375 miles to the yet-uncluttered deserts of Lassen County by special train—known locally as "The Twentieth Stenchery Limited" and "The Excess Express." The city may actually get away with this scheme, since hardly anybody lives in Lassen County except Indians, and who cares about them? But what is the answer for the metropolis that doesn't have an unspoiled desert handy?

A few ingenious notions are cropping up here and there. The Japanese are experimenting with a machine which compacts garbage, under great heat and pressure, into building blocks. A New York businessman is thinking of building a garbage mountain somewhere upstate, and equipping it with ski runs to amortize the cost. An aluminum company plans to collect and reprocess used aluminum cans—which, unlike the old-fashioned tin can, will not rust away. Our engineering department will try to Think Big along these lines. That way lies not only new careers, but salvation.

Survival U's Department of Earth Sciences will be headed—if we are lucky—by Dr. Charles F. Park, Jr., now professor of geology and mineral engineering at Stanford. He knows as well as anybody how fast mankind is using up the world's supply of raw materials. In a paper written for the American Geographical Society he punctured one of America's most engaging (and pernicious) myths: our belief that an ever-expanding economy can keep living standards rising indefinitely.

It won't happen; because, as Dr. Park demonstrates, the tonnage of metal in the earth's crust won't last indefinitely. Already we are running short of silver, mercury, tin, and cobalt—all in growing demand by the high-technology industries. Even the commoner metals may soon be in short supply. The United States alone is consuming one ton of iron and eighteen pounds of copper every year, for each of its inhabitants. Poorer countries, struggling to industrialize, hope to raise their consumption of these two key materials to something like that level. If they should succeed—and if the globe's population doubles in the next forty years, as it will at present growth rates—then the world will have to produce, somehow, *twelve times* as much iron and copper every year as it does now. Dr. Parks sees little hope that such production levels can ever

## The Entire Composition: Joining All the Parts Together 127

be reached, much less sustained indefinitely. The same thing, of course—doubled in spades—goes for other raw materials: timber, oil, natural gas, and water, to note only a few.

Survival U, therefore, will prepare its students to consume less. This does not necessarily mean an immediate drop in living standards—perhaps only a change in the yardstick by which we measure them. Conceivably Americans might be happier with fewer automobiles, neon signs, beer cans, supersonic jets, barbecue grills, and similar metallic fluff. But happy or not, our students had better learn how to live The Simpler Life, because that is what most of them are likely to have before they reach middle age.

To help them understand how very precious resources really are, our mathematics department will teach a new kind of bookkeeping: social accounting. It will train people to analyze budgets—both government and corporate—with an eye not merely to immediate dollar costs, but to the long-range costs to society.

By conventional bookkeeping methods, for example, the coal companies strip-mining away the hillsides of Kentucky and West Virginia show a handsome profit. Their ledgers, however, show only a fraction of the true cost of their operations. They take no account of destroyed land which can never bear another crop; of rivers poisoned by mud and seeping acid from the spoil banks; of floods which sweep over farms and towns downstream, because the ravaged slopes can no longer hold the rainfall. Although these costs are not borne by the mining firms, they are nevertheless real. They fall mostly on the taxpayers, who have to pay for disaster relief, flood-control levees, and the resettlement of Appalachian farm families forced off the land. As soon as our students (the taxpayers of tomorrow) learn to read a social balance sheet, they obviously will throw the strip miners into bankruptcy.

Another case study will analyze the proposal of the Inhuman Real Estate Corporation to build a fifty-story skyscraper in the most congested area of midtown Manhattan. If 90 per cent of the office space can be rented at $12 per square foot, it looks like a sound investment, according to antique accounting methods. To uncover the true facts, however, our students will investigate the cost of moving 12,000 additional workers in and out of midtown during rush hours. The first (and least) item is $8 million worth of new city buses. When they are crammed into the already clogged avenues, the daily loss of man-hours in traffic jams may run to a couple of million more. The fumes from their diesel engines will cause an estimated 9 per cent increase in New York's incidence of emphysema and lung cancer; this requires the construction of three new hospitals. To supply them, plus the new building, with water—already perilously short in the city—a new reservoir has to be built on the headwaters of the Delaware River, 140 miles away. Some of the dairy farmers pushed out of the drowned valley will move promptly into the Bronx and go on relief. The subtraction of their milk output from the city's supply leads to a price increase of two cents a quart. For a Harlem mother with seven hungry children that is the last straw. She summons her neighbors to join her in riot, seven block[s] go up in flames, and the Mayor demands higher taxes to hire more police. . . .

Instead of a sound investment, Inhuman Towers now looks like criminal folly, which would be forbidden by any sensible government. Our students will keep that in mind when they walk across campus to their government class.

Its main goal will be to discover why our institutions have done so badly in their efforts (as Dr. Falk put it) "to manage the affairs of mankind in the twentieth century." This will be a compulsory course for all freshmen, taught by professors who are capable of looking critically at every political artifact, from the Constitution to the local county council. They will start by pointing out that we are living in a state of near-anarchy, because we have no government capable of dealing effectively with public problems.

Instead we have a hodgepodge of 80,000 local governments—villages, townships, counties, cities, port authorities, sewer districts, and special purpose agencies. Their authority is so limited, and their jurisdictions so confused and overlapping, that most of them are virtually impotent. The states, which in theory could put this mess into some sort of order, usually have shown little interest and less competence. When Washington is called to help out—as it increasingly has been for the last thirty-five years—it often has proved hamhanded and entangled in its own archaic bureaucracy. The end result is that nobody in authority has been able to take care of the country's mounting needs. Our welfare rolls keep growing, our air and water get dirtier, housing gets scarcer, airports jam up, road traffic clots, railways fall apart, prices rise, ghettos burn, schools turn out more illiterates every year, and a war nobody wants drags on and on. Small wonder that so many young people are losing confidence in American institutions. In their present state, they don't deserve much confidence.

The advanced students of government at Survival U will try to find out whether these institutions can be renewed and rebuilt. They will take a hard look at the few places—Jacksonville, Minnesota, Nashville, Appalachia—which are creating new forms of government. Will these work any better, and if so, how can they be duplicated elsewhere? Can the states be brought to life, or should we start thinking about an entirely different kind of arrangement? Ten regional prefectures, perhaps, to replace the fifty states? Or should we take seriously Norman Mailer's suggestion for a new kind of city-state to govern our great metropolises? (He merely called for New York City to secede from its state; but that isn't radical enough. To be truly governable, the new Republic of New York City ought to include chunks of New Jersey and Connecticut as well.) Alternatively, can we find some way to break up Megalopolis, and spread our population into smaller and more livable communities throughout the continent? Why should we keep 70 per cent of our people crowded into less than 2 per cent of our land area, anyway?

Looking beyond our borders, our students will be encouraged to ask even harder questions. Are nation-states actually feasible, now that they have power to destroy each other in a single afternoon? Can we agree on something else to take their place, before the balance of terror becomes unstable? What price would most people be willing to pay for a more durable kind of human organization—more taxes, giving up national flags, perhaps the sacrifice of some of our hard-won liberties?

All these courses (and everything else taught at Survival U) are really branches of a single science. Human ecology is one of the youngest disciplines, and probably the most important. It is the study of the relationship between man and his environment, both natural and technological. It teaches us to understand the consequences of our actions—how sulfur-laden fuel oil burned in England produces an acid rain that damages the forest of Scandinavia, why a well-meant farm subsidy can force millions of Negro tenants off the land and lead to Watts and Hough. A graduate who comprehends ecology will know how to look at "what is going on in the world," and he will be equipped to do something about it. Whether he ends up as a city planner, a politician, an enlightened engineer, a teacher, or a reporter, he will have had a relevant education. All of its parts will hang together in a coherent whole.

And if we can get enough such graduates, man and his environment may survive a while longer, against all the odds.

*Exercise 3*

Read these two paragraphs from this speech by Malcolm X to Mississippi youth. It's good advice for all youth. This "thinking for yourself" means you choose your subject, choose your stand, and write a composition which proves it. If you can't or won't think of a problem which concerns you, skip this assignment.

One of the first things I think young people, especially nowadays, should learn is how to see for yourself and listen for yourself and think for yourself. Then you can come to an intelligent decision by yourself. If you form the habit of going by what others say about someone, or going by what others think about someone, instead of searching that thing out for yourself and seeing for yourself, you will be walking west when you think you're going east, and you will be walking east when you think you're going west. This generation, especially of our people, has a burden, more so than any other time in history. The most important thing that we can learn to do today is think for ourselves.

It's good to keep wide-open ears and listen to what everybody else has to say, but when you come to make a decision, you have to weigh all of what you've heard on its own, and place it where it belongs, and come to a decision for yourself; you'll never regret it. But if you form the habit of taking what someone else says about a thing without checking it out for yourself, you'll find that other people will have you hating your friends and loving your enemies. This is one of the things that our people are beginning to learn today—that it is very important to think out a situation for yourself. If you don't do it, you'll always be maneuvered into a situation where you are never fighting your actual enemies, where you will find yourself fighting your own self.[4]

*Exercise* 4

Newspapers print letters from their subscribers concerning community problems. Frequently, of course, such letters may express rather narrow points of view, but even sadder are the letters of concerned citizens who can't write clearly or forcefully. These letters must be brief, to the point, very clear. Try writing such a letter on some problem affecting you or your community.

*Exercise* 5

Another place where good letters could be helpful is the letter to the state legislator or Congressman. The form letter sent out by lobbies may not be very convincing; the personal, well-expressed letter may be. Citizens who complain frequently may pay little attention to this means of solving problems. Here is another chance to practice composition. Don't just write to a pretend legislator. Find the one from your district.

*Exercise* 6

Speeches or articles are given or written in praise or condemnation of an action. Would you defend or condemn those who spoke against the drafting of young men for Vietnam? Write a composition defending or condemning the action of an individual. It may be a public figure or someone you know. Quintilian's pattern for a composition applies here too.

---

[4] Malcolm X, *Malcolm X Speaks* (New York: Grove Press, Inc., 1965), pp. 137–38.

CHAPTER ELEVEN

# STYLE: AS IT RELATES TO BOTH WRITER AND READER

Style is difficult to define. Those who taught rhetoric in Greece and Rome discussed it as the choice of words, the effective arrangement of sentences, even the addition of figures of speech, always with the purpose, of course, of persuading the audience. Later periods emphasized this addition of ornament, increasing the number and emphasizing the importance of figures of speech. In the nineteenth century and during much of the twentieth, style was considered to be correct usage, although if our writers followed all the usage rules given us, we should probably describe their style as stilted, too formal, a show-off kind of writing. The rule says prepositions should not end sentences, but it seems awkward to say: For what did you go downtown?

The modern student, I think, finds the word *style* confusing because in his mind it has two associations connected with it.

One is that of changing fashion, as speedy almost as the appearance of sunshine after rain on an April day, or as slow in developing as is the growth of the child into the man and perhaps outliving more than one generation of men.

In this case it is the attention-getter that seemingly is here one moment and gone the next. It's the hula hoop, the catch phrase, the high style in dress or ornament. As hemlines go up or down, so do these fashions go in or out. This kind of fashion may demand the techniques of the assembly line, mass production from many, not the careful painstaking work of one individual.

Or there is the fashion which changes slowly; or if it seems to die out, is revived again. Thus one table is Swedish Modern; another is Victorian, its heavy dark wood reminiscent of the period of Queen Victoria.

But there is another kind of fashion, that of the master craftsman and his manner of working. When we read that it may have taken a century to build a cathedral, we learn that the father might have begun a piece of carving which his son finished. It was a slow process, each person fashioning his bit of the whole as carefully and as skillfully as his ability and training allowed. This is the painstaking fashion of the man who plants the seed and carefully nourishes the plant until the flower or fruit appears. It is the attitude of the artist, working with his oils, endeavoring to put on canvas his perceptions, his beliefs. It is the way of the poet, whose mind is filled with changing lines, always searching for the images which will best convey his idea.

Now it is this second kind of fashion which produces what we might define as style, the distinctive characteristics of composition brought about by careful thinking and writing: a choice of words to which the reader will react favorably and yet which will stimulate his imagination; freshness of figurative language, not the tired comparisons that George Orwell called "dead metaphors"; the presentation of what may be an old idea in new ways or with a new perspective or point of view.

But what, perhaps, is even more important to the student than the understanding of style is the development of his own ability. An ancient Greek teacher admitted that while he could teach almost everyone the art of rhetoric, some individuals had a natural flair. This is still true, but I find it odd that whereas no student foregoes the enjoyment of swimming just because he hasn't the talent or stamina of the Olympic Champion, he gives up the pleasure of expressing himself in words because he hasn't the flair or persistence of the few.

This competence in expression can be developed in three ways: thinking about our choice of words and sentences as described in earlier chapters; practicing exercises or keeping a journal; imitating the writing of others, not to copy but to learn techniques.

In the art museum we see students copying a picture, learning by imitation. Benjamin Franklin tells us how he did this with the essays of Addison, an English writer noted for his style. Imitation was also a part of the course in the schools of rhetoric. Their pupils did many exercises in imitation of good writers. I have found that those who read do this kind of study quite unconsciously. I remember a high school student who read all of Winston Churchill's writings and, as a result, had sentence patterns resembling Churchill's. At times I have reached the conclusion that perhaps the writers of the best compositions may owe their success less to a flair for writing than to the techniques they learned from wide reading. The Greek student did not have easy access to paperbacks, so perhaps he needed more exercises in imitation. Continual reading sharpens one's sense and appreciation of style. This doesn't mean just reading the recommended titles of a book list. Read anything. Taste changes as you proceed. The ten-year-old girl, crazy about Nancy Drew mysteries, finds their style dull at age twelve; the boy who reads at first the easiest of space fiction ends with Bradbury and Asimov.

Style was, if we return to the days of Aristotle, of three kinds: the *high,* the *middle,* and the *plain* style. In choosing his style, the speaker or writer thought of his audience or reader. The *high* style was for charming the audience, getting them emotionally involved. The language was likely to be more eloquent; the words might have more emotional associations, such as a term like "the power and the glory." High style seems less frequent today. Perhaps Winston Churchill came near to it when his speeches aroused a spirit in his people which enabled them to endure the bombing of Britain. The speeches of Frederick Douglass against slavery, although their language has a nineteenth-century flavor, probably reached the high style at times.

Poets have used it. The reader may not understand all the words Milton uses in this quotation from *Paradise Lost* when he describes Satan's fall from heaven but it is powerful.

> ... Him the Almighty Power
> Hurled headlong flaming from th' ethereal sky,
> With hideous ruin and combustion, down
> to bottomless perdition, there to dwell
> In adamantine chains and penal fire,
> Who durst defy th' Omnipotent to arms.[1]

This high style, if all emotion and no substance, might be called bombastic or florid prose. Some of those old Fourth of July orators

---
[1] John Milton, *Paradise Lost.*

used big words, gestures, and passion in delivery, but not all achieved high style.

The *middle* style is to move and persuade the audience as well as high style, but it may have fewer emotional words and a more direct appeal. A balanced sentence like this from John F. Kennedy's *Inaugural Address* was the more direct appeal of the *middle* style: "My fellow citizens of the world, ask not what America will do for you, but what together we can do for the freedom of man."

As I read the *I Have a Dream* speech of Martin Luther King, Jr., I realize its wording is that of the middle style, but when it is heard, the deep resonant tones of his voice do arouse feeling. Malcolm X, although he, too, could arouse the emotions of his audience, almost always starts with a friendly conversational tone, almost the *plain* but yet shading into middle style. After the death of our leaders, and more than one was lost in this last decade, there were many speeches. In general, I think their language was that of the middle style, although the words used did affect the listener, reminding him of his sense of loss.

The *plain* style is used for explanation of the article or speech which uses the common language of the people hearing it. I am inclined to think of this as "cookbook style: "Add the beaten yolks of two eggs and stir." Yet it may have more appeal than that. A candidate running for office, for instance, may use a middle style on some occasions, but, when speaking to the voters back home, he uses the plain speech of his home community.

Although, in earlier chapters, words and sentences were studied, up to this time we haven't mentioned figurative language, the figures of speech. These add clarity and color to writing. They are a part of everyone's language, but I almost hate to talk about them, since the background of many of you has perhaps been a lecture on similes, metaphors, and personification and the drudgery in finding them in some poem or play.

The Greek boy learned many more than these, but I suspect, like so much of that teaching, it didn't occur all at once as it so often has in our schools.

Therefore, forget if you can, the unpleasant past, and think of all the comparisons you normally use. Take your head, for example. It is more nearly round than square or rectangular. It is at the top of the body. So we use these qualities in making up words. Instead, however, of stating that just as the head is the top of the body so he is at the top of the firm, we say head man. Instead of saying a cabbage is round like the head of a man, we say head of cabbage. Legs hold us up; hence the legs of a chair or table. These are really simple metaphors. A man isn't a fox, but if he's tricky, he might be called "a sly old fox," for the fox is considered a sly, tricky animal.

Sometimes we use both elements of the comparison "He was drunk as a skunk." There, since I've never seen a drunk skunk, I imagine it is the rhyme rather than the comparison that has caused this figure of speech to last. The simile, for that is what it is, can provide freshness and color in writing. The England described by P. G. Wodehouse is different today; his plots are out-of-date; yet his writing is still popular with many, perhaps because of his use of similes. I might say: He sputtered like a boiling coffee pot. His attitude was feverish. Wodehouse says of the man's manner: "a sort of fizzing and bubbling like that of a coffee pot about to come to the height of its fever."

Of the cross tone of a man's voice, he states: "It fell somewhat short of the snarl of a timber wolf which has hurt its shinbone on a passing rock, but it was not enthusiastic and genial."

We use personification, too, giving inanimate things like thunder the power to roar or the wind to whistle. The difficulty lies in finding new comparisons, but this, as Chapter One suggested, simply means closer observation, seeing a similarity of one relationship between different things. Done in a fresh way they add to writing.

Of course, I realize that you may consider style as no more necessary than the chrome on a car. But it is more than that. Oatmeal, though nourishing, tastes better with sugar and cream, and our writing is often more appealing with an occasional figure of speech. It's the jam on the bread, to use a homely metaphor.

We also need to recognize style because it can influence us. Hitler's emotional style, playing upon love of country, fear, and the feeling of an unjust past, led many an unthinking listener to become involved in another war. We need to recognize when style has substance, whether it is encouraging us to do the right action or whether it urges us to disregard the right and do the wrong. To judge we must know.

We may not get beyond the plain style, yet what we say can be clear and, if we desire to be even more effective, we may even find it desirable to do a bit of polishing. The inspired sentence is rare; the revised one is common. The following are revisions in John F. Kennedy's *Inaugural Address*. As you can see, he did not trust inspiration.

### INAUGURAL ADDRESS OF JOHN F. KENNEDY[2]

| First Draft | Next-to-Last Draft | Last Draft |
| --- | --- | --- |
| We celebrate today not a victory of party but the sacrament of democracy. | We celebrate today not a victory of party but a convention of freedom. | We observe today not a victory of party but a celebration of freedom. |
| Each of us, whether we hold office or not, shares the responsibility for guiding this most difficult of all societies along the path of self-discipline and government. | In your hands, my fellow citizens, more than in mine, will be determined the success or failure of our course. | In your hands, my fellow citizens, more than mine, will rest the final success or failure of our course. |
| Nor can two great and powerful nations forever continue on this reckless course, both overburdened by the staggering cost of modern weapons. | . . . neither can two great and powerful nations long endure their present reckless course, both overburdened by the staggering cost of modern weapons. | . . . neither can two great and powerful groups of nations take comfort from our present course—both sides overburdened by the cost of modern weapons . . . |

### TWO SENTENCES FROM EARLIER SPEECHES WHICH GAVE SUGGESTIONS FOR THE *INAUGURAL ADDRESS*[3]

. . . It is time, in short, for a new generation of Americans.

. . . the torch has been passed to a new generation of Americans.

We do not campaign stressing what our country is going to do for us as a people. We stress what we can do for the country, for all of us.

And so, my fellow Americans, ask not what your country can do for you; ask what you can do for your country.

---

[2] Theodore C. Sorensen, *Kennedy* (New York: Harper and Row, 1965), pp. 241–42.
[3] *Ibid.*

*Exercise* 1

Study these revisions. Then discuss these questions.

*a.* Why did he discard "sacrament" and "convention" for "celebration"?

*b.* Why was the phrase "whether we hold office or not" omitted?

*c.* Why was the idea of "enduring" or "continuing" on this "reckless course" changed to "take comfort from our present course"?

*d.* Since the cost of weapons is "staggering" to contemplate, why omit this word?

*e.* Why use the term "the torch has been passed"? What does this suggest? Where or when is this done?

*f.* The last quotation "We do not campaign stressing . . ." has two declarative statements. What is the reason for changing these into what we call a balanced sentence (The Greek word was, and we still use it, antithesis.)?

*Exercise* 2

A good way to understand style is to compare that of several authors who are writing the same kind of story. Mickey Spillane simply has the hero kill someone and get the girl, with much blood and no development of character.

The hero of Ian Fleming's novels also engages in combat; he also gets the girl; but he is a more sophisticated character. He can enjoy the evening breeze, the flowers in a hotel garden, the charm of well-prepared food.

But in the spy novels of John Buchan, the hero becomes more than a figurehead to outwit the enemy. Buchan knew history; he loved his country, particularly Scotland. These facts make his spy stories more logical, his characters more like real human beings.

Students who read many of the stories classified as science fiction find that certain authors have definite styles. It is rather like a game to pick up a book and, without reading an author's name, know who wrote it.

If you have read several books by one author, try to list the characteristics of his style.

*Exercise* 2

Read the following descriptions. Which author's style do you prefer? Why? If you dislike all of them, then state your reasons.

*a.* I could have made short work and landed at Hull but I would not:

I was so afraid. For I was used to the silence of the ice; and I was used to the silence of the sea: but I was afraid of the silence of England.[4]

*b.* Ralph Kabnis, propped in his bed, tries to read. To read himself to sleep. An oil lamp on a chair near his elbow burns unsteadily. The cabin room is spaced fantastically about it. Whitewashed hearth and chimney, black with sooty saw teeth. Ceiling patterned by the fringed globe of the lamp. The walls, unpainted, are seasoned a rosin yellow. And cracks between the boards are black. These cracks are the lips the night winds use for whispering. Night winds in Georgia are vagrant poets, whispering.[5]

*c.* The unicorn lived in a lilac wood, and she lived all alone. She was very old, though she did not know it, and she was no longer the careless color of sea foam, but rather the color of snow falling on a moonlit night. But her eyes were still clear and unwearied, and she still moved like a shadow on the sea.[6]

*d.* It was a large, handsome, stone building, standing well on rising ground, and backed by a ridge of high woody hills;—and in front, a stream of some natural importance was swelled into greater, but without any artificial appearance. Its banks were neither formal, nor falsely adorned.[7]

*Exercise 4*

Check the style of writing in two of your textbooks. Is it clear? Does it arouse the reader's interest? If your answer is yes to both of these questions, then try to see how the author accomplishes this. If the answer has been a negative one, then suggest how the style could be changed. Why might textbook authors have a style different from that of the fiction writer?

*Exercise 5*

Bring to class a sentence you have read, or heard, that seems to you to have style. Discuss these sentences in class.

*Exercise 6*

This exercise can be helpful even if you don't achieve success. Write one paragraph upon some aspect of pollution in the *plain* style, the one

[4] M. P. Shiel, *The Purple Cloud* (New York: The Vanguard Press, 1930), p. 78.
[5] Jean Toomer, *Cane* (New York: Harper & Row, 1969), p. 157.
[6] Peter S. Beagle, *The Last Unicorn* (New York: Ballentine Books, Inc., 1969), p. 1.
[7] Jane Austen, *Pride and Prejudice* (Boston: Houghton Mifflin Company, 1956), p. 181.

we commonly use. Then try to redo the paragraph in *middle* style, and finally in *high* style.

Here is an example of just one sentence, in each style.

*Plain.* The landscape is marred by masses of junked cars.

*Middle.* Our countryside is covered with literally acres of junked cars, destroying the beauty of acres that may soon be necessary for pasture, planting, or recreation; and the prospect, at least at present, leads one to believe even more land will be so covered in the future.

*High.* No longer can our children be led through green pastures beside the still waters, no longer need they learn to lift up their voices to praise the beauty of the earth, God's gift to man, for no plague of locusts could be more destructive to our fertile acres than this plague of discarded cars, these hulking masses of ugly metal, making a mockery of *America, the Beautiful*. (Perhaps you can do better working together on the paragraph of high style, for I found it difficult to do just one sentence. We are not accustomed to speaking or writing in the high style, but a touch of it now and then may be more persuasive.)

CHAPTER TWELVE

# READING FOR IDEAS: LOOKING FOR A SUBJECT

Trying to find a subject may occasionally seem as useless as looking for the proverbial "needle in a haystack." Our mind seems to be blank, or if an idea does come to us it is about as clear as a dirty windshield. Perhaps what we need to do is to "prime the pump." In the days when wells were common, the thirsty person might work the pump handle up and down but get no water. But if he poured water into the top of the pump, worked the handle again, water gushed out. There is probably a simple scientific reason for this, but, what was most important, it worked.

Now one way of priming your mind is to pour into it something someone else has said, but you have to read this material in a certain way, not saying to yourself, "What facts will I be asked about this on a text?" but "What do I think about this? How does it apply to my life? Do I think this way? Would these ideas be true today?"

Then, after reading in this way, forming your opinions, answers to these questions should be discussed in class, for what other students have to say may intensify, broaden, modify your ideas, or even give you new ones. I remember when a class of mine was reading a chapter from Thoreau's *Walden,* a product of an early nineteenth-century American writer. At first, as often happens, when students read what English teachers have rather priggishly termed "good literature," the class wasn't very enthusiastic. Here was a man who thought railroads ruined the countryside, who insisted that he could find enough to see and do in his own vicinity without traveling elsewhere, who believed that men had become "the tool of their tools," that there is an "illusion" about modern improvements.

But even knowing all these beliefs of the author wasn't getting us toward subjects for writing. Then someone suggested that it would be hard for a man like Thoreau to lead his independent life today. This started the debate. Did we have to conform? Could we be independent? Did we slave away to get material things and have no time to enjoy them? It was in this way that the class interpreted "the tool of their tools." Some even took "Men are the tool of their tools." as their thesis statement for a composition.

What happened during this discussion was that the students observed the relationship between Thoreau and his ideas and how they applied or did not apply to their lives. Yet, if I had just asked them to write a composition, perhaps none of these subjects would have occurred to them. This reading also gave them another source of material, Thoreau's beliefs, to add to experiences from their own lives.

This is the value of reading to stimulate our thought processes. Therefore, this chapter contains five pieces of writing, each of which, after reading and discussing, should give a subject for a composition. But, again, the warning: Get your thesis statement clear before tackling the writing. It helps, as I have suggested before, to write this statement out and keep it in sight, like the housewife I know who, after moving to a strange city, learned her way around in a very short time by putting up a city map over the sink and studying it while she did the dishes.

## A

After reading the following speech, try writing a short paper proving one of the following thesis statements; or if you think of one of your own, so much the better.

*Note:* Before choosing or writing, there should be discussion of the speech in class. Nineteenth century writing is not always easy reading.

1. Frederick Douglass follows the rhetorical principles for a ceremonial speech in high style. (You will be writing mainly a composition of analysis and explanation.)

2. The ideas of Frederick Douglass are still true. (Proof will be your observations as applied to the points Douglass makes.)

3. The situation Douglass describes should not continue.

4. Our nation does have "national inconsistencies."

Here is the speech, delivered at Corinthian Hall, Rochester, July 5, 1852. This custom of a ceremonial speech to commemorate a special occasion such as the Fourth of July was a popular one for many years. At the time Douglass delivered it, the country was involved in a controversy over slavery. Frederick Douglass, a former slave, had escaped to the North and was an abolitionist. (He studied the art of rhetoric on his own after he was past high school age.)

## No Day of Triumph[1]

The Fourth of July evoked no enthusiasm among abolitionists; they held that it was inconsistent to celebrate independence and freedom in a land in which slavery existed. Douglass shared this view, preferring to let the day pass in silence. However, when he was invited by the Rochester Ladies' Anti-Slavery Society to deliver the Fourth of July oration in 1852, he made the most of the occasion. His speech was not devoted to patriotic themes but addressed itself to the question, "What, to the American slave, is your Fourth of July?"

The papers and placards say that I am to deliver a Fourth of July Oration. This certainly sounds large, and out of the common way, for me. It is true that I have often had the privilege to speak in this beautiful Hall, and to address many who now honor me with their presence. But neither their familiar faces, nor the perfect gage I think I have of Corinthian Hall seems to free me from embarrassment.

The fact is, ladies and gentlemen, the distance between this platform and the slave plantation, from which I escaped, is considerable—and the difficulties to be overcome in getting from the latter to the former are by no means slight. That I am here to-day is, to me, a matter of astonishment as well as of gratitude. You will not, therefore, be surprised, if in what I have to say I evince no elaborate preparation, nor grace my speech with any high sounding exordium. With little experience and with less learning, I have been able to throw my thoughts hastily and imperfectly together; and trusting to your patient and generous indulgence, I will proceed to lay them before you.

This, for the purpose of this celebration, is the Fourth of July. It is the

---

[1] Frederick Douglass, in *Great Lives Observed*, edited by Benjamin Quarles (Englewood Cliffs, N.J.: Prentice Hall, Inc., 1968), pp. 44–49.

birthday of your National Independence, and of your political freedom. This, to you, is what the Passover was to the emancipated people of God. It carries your minds back to the day, and to the act of your great deliverance; and to the signs, and to the wonders, associated with that act, and that day. This celebration also marks the beginning of another year of your national life; and reminds you that the Republic of America is now 76 years old. I am glad, fellow-citizens, that your nation is so young. Seventy-six years, though a good old age for a man, is but a mere speck in the life of a nation. Three score years and ten is the allotted time for individual men; but nations number their years by thousands. According to this fact, you are, even now, only in the beginning of your national career, still lingering in the period of childhood. I repeat, I am glad this is so. There is hope in the thought, and hope is much needed, under the dark clouds which lower above the horizon. The eye of the reformer is met with angry flashes, portending disastrous times; but his heart may well beat lighter at the thought that America is young, and that she is still in the impressible stage of her existence. May he not hope that high lessons of wisdom, of justice and of truth, will yet give direction to her destiny? Were the nation older, the patriot's heart might be sadder, and the reformer's brow heavier. Its future might be shrouded in gloom, and the hope of its prophets go out in sorrow. There is consolation in the thought that America is young.—Great streams are not easily turned from channels, worn deep in the course of ages. They may sometimes rise in quiet and stately majesty, and inundate the land, refreshing and fertilizing the earth with their mysterious properties. They may also rise in wrath and fury, and bear away, on their angry waves, the accumulated wealth of years of toil and hardship. They, however, gradually flow back to the same old channel, and flow on as serenely as ever. But, while the river may not be turned aside, it may dry up, and leave nothing behind but the withered branch, and the unsightly rock, to howl in the abyss-sweeping wind, the sad tale of departed glory. As with rivers so with nations....

Fellow-citizens, pardon me, allow me to ask, why am I called upon to speak here to-day? What have I, or those I represent, to do with your national independence? Are the great principles of political freedom and of natural justice, embodied in that Declaration of Independence, extended to us? and am I, therefore, called upon to bring our humble offering to the national altar, and to confess the benefits and express devout gratitude for the blessings resulting from your independence to us?

Would to God, both for your sakes and ours, that an affirmative answer could be truthfully returned to these questions! Then would my task be light, and my burden easy and delightful. For *who* is there so cold, that a nation's sympathy could not warm him? Who so obdurate and dead to the claims of gratitude, that would not thankfully acknowledge such priceless benefits? Who so stolid and selfish, that would not give his voice to swell the hallelujahs of a nation's jubilee, when the chains of servitude had been torn from his limbs? I am not that man. In a case like that, the dumb might eloquently speak, and the "lame man leap as an hart."

But such is not the state of the case. I say it with a sad sense of disparity between us. I am not included within the pale of this glorious anniversary! Your high independence only reveals the immeasurable distance between us. The blessings in which you, this day, rejoice, are not enjoyed in common.— The rich inheritance of justice, liberty, prosperity and independence, bequeathed by your fathers, is shared by you, not by me. The sunlight that brought light and healing to you, has brought stripes and death to me. This Fourth of July is *yours,* not *mine. You* may rejoice, *I* must mourn. To drag a man in fetters into the grand illuminated temple of liberty, and call upon him to join you in joyous anthems, were inhuman mockery and sacrilegious irony. Do you mean, citizens, to mock me, by asking me to speak to-day? If so, there is a parallel to your conduct. And let me warn you that it is dangerous to copy the example of a nation whose crimes, towering up to heaven, were thrown down by the breath of the Almighty, burying that nation in irrevocable ruin! I can to-day take up the plaintive lament of a peeled and woe-smitten people! . . .

What, to the American slave, is your 4th of July? I answer; a day that reveals to him, more than all other days in the year, the gross injustice and cruelty to which he is the constant victim. To him, your celebration is a sham; your boasted liberty, an unholy license; your national greatness, swelling vanity; your sounds of rejoicing are empty and heartless; your denunciation of tyrants, brass fronted impudence; your shouts of liberty and equality, hollow mockery; your prayers and hymns, your sermons and thanksgivings, with all your religious parade and solemnity, are, to him, mere bombast, fraud, deception, impiety, and hypocrisy—a thin veil to cover up crimes which would disgrace a nation of savages. There is not a nation on the earth guilty of practices more shocking and bloody than are the people of the United States, at this very hour.

Go where you may, search where you will, roam through all the monarchies and despotisms of the Old World, travel through South America, search out every abuse, and when you have found the last, lay your facts by the side of the everyday practices of this nation, and you will say with me, that, for revolting barbarity and shameless hypocrisy, America reigns without a rival. . . .

Americans! your republican politics, not less than your republican religion, are flagrantly inconsistent. You boast of your love of liberty, your superior civilization, and your pure Christianity, while the whole political power of the nation (as embodied in the two great political parties) is solemnly pledged to support and perpetuate the enslavement of three millions of your countrymen. You hurl your anathemas at the crowned headed tyrants of Russia and Austria and pride yourselves on your Democratic institutions, while you yourselves consent to be the mere *tools* and *body-guards* of the tyrants of Virginia and Carolina. You invite to your shores fugitives of oppression from abroad, honor them with banquets, greet them with ovations, cheer them, toast them, salute them, protect them, and pour out your money to them like water; but the fugitives from your own land you advertise, hunt, arrest, shoot, and kill. You glory in your refinement and your universal education; yet you maintain a system as barbarous and dreadful as ever stained the character of a nation—a system begun in avarice, supported in pride, and perpetuated in cruelty. You shed tears over fallen Hungary, and make the sad story of her wrongs the theme of your poets, statesmen, and orators, till your gallant sons are ready to fly to arms to vindicate her cause against the oppressor; but, in regard to the ten thousand wrongs of the American slave, you would enforce the strictest silence, and would hail him as an enemy of the nation who dares to make those wrongs the subject of public discourse! You are all on fire at the mention of liberty for France or for Ireland; but are as cold as an iceberg at the thought of liberty for the enslaved of America. You discourse eloquently on the dignity of labor; yet, you sustain a system which, in its very essence, casts a stigma upon labor. You can bare your bosom to the storm of British artillery to throw off a three-penny tax on tea; and yet wring the last hard earned farthing from the grasp of the black laborers of your country. You profess to believe "that, of one blood, God made all nations of men to dwell on the face of all the earth," and hath commanded all men, everywhere, to love one another; yet you notoriously hate (and glory in your hatred) all men whose skins are not colored like your own. You declare before the world, and are understood by the world to declare that you *"hold these truths to be self-evident, that all men are created equal; and are endowed by their Creator with certain inalienable rights; and that among these are, life, liberty, and the pursuit of happiness";* and yet, you hold securely, in a bondage which, according to your own Thomas Jefferson, *"is worse than ages of that which your fathers rose in rebellion to oppose,"* a seventh part of the inhabitants of your country.

Fellow-citizens, I will not enlarge further on your national inconsistencies. The existence of slavery in this country brands your republicanism as a sham, your humanity as a base pretense, and your Christianity as a lie. It destroys your moral power abroad: it corrupts your politicians at home. It saps the foundation of religion; it makes your name a hissing and a bye-word to a mocking earth. It is the antagonistic force in your government, the only thing that seriously disturbs and endangers your *Union*. It fetters your progress; it is the enemy of improvement; the deadly foe of education; it fosters pride; it breeds insolence; it promotes vice; it shelters crime; it is a curse to the earth that supports it; and yet you cling to it as if it were the sheet anchor of all your hopes. Oh! be warned! be warned! a horrible reptile is coiled up in your nation's bosom; the venomous creature is nursing at the tender breast of your youthful republic; *for the love of God, tear away,* and fling from you the hideous monster, and *let the weight of twenty millions crush and destroy it forever!* ...

Allow me to say, in conclusion, notwithstanding the dark picture I have this day presented, of the state of the nation, I do not despair of this country. There are forces in operation which must inevitably work the downfall of slavery. "The arm of the Lord is not shortened," and the doom of slavery is certain. I, therefore, leave off where I began, with hope. While drawing encouragement from "the Declaration of Independence," the great principles it contains, and the genius of American institutions, my spirit is also cheered by the obvious tendencies of the age. Nations do not now stand in the same relation to each other that they did ages ago. No nation can now shut itself up from the surrounding world and trot round in the same old path of its fathers without interference. The time was when such could be done. Long established customs of hurtful character could formerly fence themselves in, and do their evil work with social impunity. Knowledge was then confined and enjoyed by the privileged few, and the multitude walked on in mental darkness. But a change has now come over the affairs of mankind. Walled cities and empires have become unfashionable. The arm of commerce has borne away the gates of the strong city. Intelligence is penetrating the darkest corners of the globe. It makes its pathway over and under the sea, as well as on the earth. Wind, steam, and lightning are its chartered agents. Oceans no longer divide, but link nations together. From Boston to London is now a holiday excursion. Space is comparatively annihilated. Thoughts expressed on one side of the Atlantic are distinctly heard on the other.

The far off and almost fabulous Pacific rolls in grandeur at our feet. The Celestial Empire, the mystery of ages, is being solved. The fiat of the Almighty, "Let there be Light," has not yet spent its force. No abuse, no outrage whether in taste, sport or avarice, can now hide itself from the all-pervading light. The iron shoe, and crippled foot of China must be seen in contrast with nature. Africa must rise and put on her yet unwoven garment. "Ethiopia shall stretch out her hand unto God." In the fervent aspirations of William Lloyd Garrison, I say, and let every heart join in saying it:

*God speed the year of jubilee*
*The wide world o'er!*

# B

This next speech is by James Baldwin, a twentieth century writer. Like Douglass, he is involved in the racial problem, but his style differs. His language is probably more easily understood, but discussion before choosing a topic or writing will still be practical. Choose one of these topics or create your own for your composition.

1. Baldwin and Douglass present different aspects of the racial problem.
2. Baldwin suggests that people do not do as they wish to do because they are afraid. (Here is a good idea for a composition, since you must know examples of people giving in to their fear. On the other hand, you could discuss those who went ahead despite their fears.)
3. "The world is before you and you need not take it or leave it as it was before you came in." (This is a good subject for writing. But you might narrow it a bit by indicating that by improving his own segment of the world, the person adds to the betterment of others.
4. Do you think we can, as Baldwin suggests, "create a world in which there are no minorities"? How could we go about it? Are we? What signs do you see of change? (This might make an interesting subject.)
5. Baldwin uses specific examples to prove his points.

This speech by James Baldwin was delivered at Kalamazoo College. The date was probably around 1960.

## In Search of a Majority[2]

### An Address

I am supposed to speak this evening on the goals of American society as they involve minority rights, but what I am really going to do is to invite you to join me in a series of speculations. Some of them are dangerous, some of them painful, all of them are reckless. It seems to me that before we can begin to speak of minority rights in this country, we've got to make some attempt to isolate or to define the majority.

Presumably the society in which we live is an expression—in some way—of the majority will. But it is not so easy to locate this majority. The moment one attempts to define this majority one is faced with several conundrums. Majority is not an expression of numbers, of numerical strength, for example. You may far outnumber your opposition and not be able to impose your will on them or even to modify the rigor with which they impose their will on you, i.e., the Negroes in South Africa or in some counties, some sections, of the American South. You may have beneath your hand all the apparatus of power, political, military, state, and still be unable to use these things to achieve your ends, which is the problem faced by de Gaulle in Algeria and the problem which faced Eisenhower when, largely because of his own inaction, he was forced to send paratroopers into Little Rock. Again, the most trenchant observers of the scene in the South, those who are embattled there, feel that the Southern mobs are not an expression of the Southern majority will. Their impression is that these mobs fill, so to speak, a moral vacuum and that the people who form these mobs would be very happy to be released from their pain, and their ignorance, if someone arrived to show them the way. I would be inclined to agree with this, simply from what we know of human nature. It is not my impression that people wish to become worse; they really wish to become better but very often do not know how. Most people assume the position, in a way, of the Jews in Egypt, who really wished to get to the Promised Land but were afraid of the rigors of the journey; and, of course, before you embark on a journey the terrors

---

[2] James Baldwin, "In Search of a Majority," *Nobody Knows My Name* (New York: Dell Publishing Co., 1960), pp. 107–14.

of whatever may overtake you on that journey live in the imagination and paralyze you. It was through Moses, according to legend, that they discovered, by undertaking this journey, how much they could endure.

These speculations have led me a little bit ahead of myself. I suppose it can be said that there was a time in this country when an entity existed which could be called the majority, let's say a class, for the lack of a better word, which created the standards by which the country lived or which created the standards to which the country aspired. I am referring to or have in mind, perhaps somewhat arbitrarily, the aristocracies of Virginia and New England. These were mainly of Anglo-Saxon stock and they created what Henry James was to refer to, not very much later, as our Anglo-American heritage, or Anglo-American connections. Now at no time did these men ever form anything resembling a popular majority. Their importance was that they kept alive and they bore witness to two elements of a man's life which are not greatly respected among us now: (1) the social forms, called manners, which prevent us from rubbing too abrasively against one another and (2) the interior life, or the life of the mind. These things were important; these things were realities for them and no matter how rough-hewn or dark the country was then, it is important to remember that this was also the time when people sat up in log cabins studying very hard by lamplight or candlelight. That they were better educated than we are now can be proved by comparing the political speeches of that time with those of our own day.

Now, what I have been trying to suggest in all this is that the only useful definition of the word "majority" does not refer to numbers, and it does not refer to power. It refers to influence. Someone said, and said it very accurately, that what is honored in a country is cultivated there. If we apply this touchstone to American life we can scarcely fail to arrive at a very grim view of it. But I think we have to look grim facts in the face because if we don't, we can never hope to change them.

These vanished aristocracies, these vanished standard bearers, had several limitations, and not the least of these limitations was the fact that their standards were essentially nostalgic. They referred to a past condition; they referred to the achievements, the laborious achievements, of a stratified society; and what was evolving in America had nothing to do with the past. So inevitably what happened, putting it far too simply, was that the old forms gave way before the European tidal wave, gave way before the rush of Italians, Greeks, Spaniards, Irishmen, Poles, Persians, Norwegians, Swedes, Danes, wandering Jews from every nation under heaven, Turks, Armenians, Lithuanians, Japanese, Chinese, and Indians. Everybody was here suddenly in the melting pot, as we like to say, but without any intention of being melted. They were here because they had wanted to leave wherever they had been and they were here to make their lives, and achieve their futures, and to establish a new identity. I doubt if history has ever seen such a spectacle, such a conglomeration of hopes, fears, and desires. I suggest, also, that they presented a problem for the Puritan God, who had never heard of them and of whom they had never heard. Almost always as they arrived, they took their places as a minority, a minority because their influence was so slight and because it was their necessity to make themselves over in the image of their new and unformed country. There were no longer any universally accepted forms or standards, and since all the roads to the achievement of an identity had vanished, the problem of status in American life became and it remains today acute. In a way, status became a kind of substitute for identity, and because money and the things money can buy is the universally accepted symbol here of status, we are often condemned as materialists. In fact, we are much closer to being metaphysical because nobody has ever expected from things the miracles that we expect.

Now I think it will be taken for granted that the Irish, the Swedes, the Danes, etc., who came here can no longer be considered in any serious way as minorities; and the question of anti-Semitism presents too many special features to be profitably discussed here tonight. The American minorities can be placed on a kind of color wheel. For example, when we think of the American boy, we don't usually think of a Spanish, Turkish, a Greek, or a Mexican type, still less of an Oriental type. We usually think of someone who is kind of a cross between the Teuton and the Celt, and I think it is interesting to consider what this image suggests. Outrageous as this image is, in most cases, it is the national self-image. It is an image which suggests hard work and good clean fun and chastity and piety and success. It leaves out of account, of course, most of the people in the country, and most of the facts of life, and there is not much point in discussing those virtues it suggests, which are mainly honored in the breach. The point is that it has almost nothing to do with what or who an American really is. It has nothing to do with what life is. Beneath this bland, this conqueror image, a great many unadmitted despairs and confusions, and anguish and unadmitted crimes and failures hide. To speak in my own person, as a member of the nation's most oppressed minority, the oldest oppressed minority, I want to suggest most seriously that before we can do very much in the way of clear thinking or clear doing as relates in the minorities in this country, we must first crack the American image and find out and deal with what it hides. We cannot discuss the state of our minorities until we first have some sense of what we are, who we are, what our goals are, and what we take life to be. The question is not what we can do now for the hypothetical Mexican, the hypothetical Negro. The question is what we really want out of life, for ourselves, what we think is real.

Now I think there is a very good reason why the Negro in this country has been treated for such a long time in such a cruel way, and some of the reasons are economic and some of them are political. We have discussed these reasons without ever coming to any kind of resolution for a very long time. Some of them are social, and these reasons are somewhat more important because they have to do with our social panic, with our fear of losing status. This really amounts sometimes to a kind of social paranoia. One cannot afford to lose status on this peculiar ladder, for the prevailing notion of American life seems to involve a kind of rung-by-rung ascension to some hideously desirable state. If this is one's concept of life, obviously one cannot afford to slip back one rung. When one slips, one slips back not a rung but back into chaos and no longer knows who he is. And this reason, this fear, suggests to me one of the real reasons for the status of the Negro in this country. In a way, the Negro tells us where the bottom is: *because he is there,* and *where* he is, beneath us, we know where the limits are and how far we must not fall. We must not fall beneath him. We must never allow ourselves to fall that low, and I am not trying to be cynical or sardonic. I think if one examines the myths which have proliferated in this country concerning the Negro, one discovers beneath these myths a kind of sleeping terror of some condition which we refuse to imagine. In a way, if the Negro were not here, we might be forced to deal within ourselves and our own personalities, with all those vices, all those conundrums, and all those mysteries with which we have invested the Negro race. Uncle Tom is, for example, if he is called uncle, a kind of saint. He is there, he endures, he will forgive us, and this is a key to that image. But if he is not uncle, if he is merely Tom, he is a danger to everybody. He will wreak havoc on the countryside. When he is Uncle Tom he has no sex—when he is Tom, he does—and this obviously says much more about the people who invented this myth than it does about the people who are the object of it.

If you have been watching television lately, I think this is unendurably clear in the faces of those screaming people in the South, who are quite incapable of telling you what it is they are afraid of. They do not really know what it is they are afraid of, but they know they are afraid of something, and they are so frightened that they are nearly out of their minds. And this same fear obtains on one level or another, to varying degrees, throughout the entire country. We would never, never allow Negroes to starve, to grow bitter, and to die in ghettos all over the country if we were not driven by some nameless fear that has nothing to do with Negroes. We would never victimize, as we do, children whose only crime is color and keep them, as we put it, in their place. We wouldn't drive Negroes mad as we do by accepting them in ball parks, and on concert stages, but not in our homes and not in our neighborhoods, and not in our churches. It is only too clear that even with the most malevolent will in the world Negroes can never manage to achieve one-tenth of the harm which we fear. No, it has everything to do with ourselves and this is one of the reasons that for all these generations we have disguised this problem in the most incredible jargon. One of the reasons we are so fond of sociological reports and research and investigational committees is because they hide something. As long as we can deal with the Negro as a kind of statistic, as something to be manipulated, something to be fled from, or something to be given something to, there is something we can avoid, and what we can avoid is what he really, really means to us. The question that still ends these discussions is an extraordinary question: Would you let your sister marry one? The question, by the way, depends on several extraordinary assumptions. First of all it assumes, if I may say so, that I *want* to marry your sister and it also assumes that if I asked your sister to marry me, she would immediately say yes. There is no reason to make either of these assumptions, which are clearly irrational, and the key to why these assumptions are held is not to be found by asking Negroes. The key to why these assumptions are held has something to do with some insecurity in the people who hold them. It is only, after all, too clear that everyone born is going to have a rather difficult time getting through his life. It is only too clear that people fall in love according to some principle that we have not as yet been able to define, to discover or to isolate, and that marriage depends entirely on the two people involved; so that this objection does not hold water. It certainly is not justification for segregated schools or for ghettos or for mobs. I suggest that the role of the Negro in American life has something to do with our concept of what God is, and from my point of view, this concept is not big enough. It has got to be made much bigger than it is because God is, after all, not anybody's toy. To be with God is really to be involved with some enormous, overwhelming desire, and joy, and power which you cannot control, which controls you. I conceive of my own life as a journey toward something I do not understand, which in the going toward, makes me better. I conceive of God, in fact, as a means of liberation and not a means to control others. Love does not begin and end the way we seem to think it does. Love is a battle, love is a war; love is a growing up. No one in the world—in the entire world—knows more—knows Americans better or, odd as this may sound, loves them more than the American Negro. This is because he has had to watch you, outwit you, deal with you, and bear you, and sometimes even bleed and die with you, ever since we got here, that is, since both of us, black and white, got here—and this is a wedding. Whether I like it or not, or whether you like it or not, we are bound together forever. We are part of each other. What is happening to every Negro in the country at any time is also happening to you. There is no way around this. I am suggesting that these walls—these artificial walls—which have been up so long to protect us from something we fear, must come down. I think that what we really have to do is to create a country in which there are no minorities—for the first time in the history of the world. The one thing that all Americans have in common is that they have no other identity apart from the identity which is being achieved on this continent. This is not the English necessity, or the Chinese necessity, or the French necessity, but they are born into a framework which allows them their identity. The necessity of Americans to achieve an identity is a historical and a present personal fact and this is the connection between you and me.

This brings me back, in a way, to where I started. I said that we couldn't talk about minorities until we had talked about majorities, and I also said that majorities had nothing to do with numbers or with power, but with influence, with moral influence, and I want to suggest this: that the majority for which everyone is seeking which must reassess and release us from our past and deal with the present and create standards worthy of what a man may be—this majority is you. No one else can do it. The world is before you and you need not take it or leave it as it was when you came in.

## C

This article may bring almost too many ideas to mind, since the mention of the deterioration of train service makes us think of other problems of transportation: traffic jams, crowded buses and subways, miles of cement, the noise of jets, and the price of travel. If none of this bothers you, then you are more fortunate than most of us. Right now I could write on this thesis statement: My community needs better transportation. Perhaps this would be a good subject for your composition.

### *One Helluva Way to Run a Railroad*[3]

Or: Will "the vanishing American" ever
again find happiness riding the rails?

I might as well begin by admitting that I am a man of peculiar tastes in transportation. In the first place, I like to relax when I am going somewhere, which immediately puts me in the oddball corner. I also like to be able to get up and walk around in transit, without interrupting the transit. I like to eat at my leisure, at a time of my choice, and I prefer to sit at a table when I do so. I even enjoy looking at scenery! And I like at least a relative degree of safety while I travel. In short, I like to ride the railroads. I realize that all this puts me seriously out of step with most of my contemporaries, who seem to prefer to be jammed in somewhere and hustled to their destinations with their eyes either on the road or on the clouds. In fact, the other day I read an ad which described me as "the vanishing American."

This description was interesting, but even more interesting was the source—*a railroad!* It seemed a little odd that a railroad was spending its hard-earned (or hard-lost?) money to convince me that I am obsolete, and, in effect, was saying, "Get lost, brother." I had heard, as has everyone else, that railroads have come upon hard times, and I decided to find out just what railroads were up against, and how good my chances were of

---

[3] Elmo Roper, "One Helluva Way To Run A Railroad," *Saturday Review* (June 28, 1969), pp. 18, 19.

their survival. Some of the things I discovered I had suspected, but others came as a surprise; together they made up a picture of the railroads that differed considerably from the image that is currently popular.

The current characterization of the plight of railroads vis-à-vis passengers runs something like this: Railroad passenger service is a hopelessly uneconomic operation for three principal reasons: 1) people don't want to ride railroads any more; 2) competitive forms of transportation such as airlines and highways benefit from subsidies and tax advantages which railroads do not have; and 3) unions have forced on the railroads inefficient and expensive labor practices and regulations. The inevitable conclusion: Railroad passenger service is obsolete, and most of it will eventually have to disappear.

This is the picture, and it contains some elements of truth. But if one goes a little further, a very different picture emerges. To put it bluntly, it is a picture of railroad management actively engaged in the process of digging its own grave—or at least the grave of passenger service. To begin with, one of the reasons people don't want to ride the railroads any more is that railroads are actively discouraging them from doing so. Trains are dirty, stations are poorly maintained, and the number of ticket windows is often reduced so that one has to stand endlessly in line to buy a ticket, or they are closed down completely when one arrives. The quality of food has gone down, while prices for it have gone up. There is virtually no promotion or advertising of passenger service; in fact, it is not uncommon to read ads like the one I ran across suggesting that those who persist on riding the rails are curious relics of a bygone era. Under such circumstances, it is a wonder, not that there aren't more of us, but that there are any railroad passengers left at all.

It is true that railroads are at a competitive disadvantage with highways and airlines, because they own and are taxed on their facilities, while highway and air facilities are paid for by public agencies, which are not fully reimbursed by "user charges." Railroads have made efforts to get their taxes reduced—which, in view of the pressures on localities to produce more tax revenue, have little chance of succeeding—but they have shown a marked resistance to more imaginative approaches to the problem. For example, the suggestion has been made that the Government acquire fixed railroad facilities and lease them back to the railroads, thus eliminating their tax disadvantages at a stroke. This proposal is greeted by railroad management with horror, out of a fear of losing their right to run their own railroad, or worse, of losing the right to make profits from their real estate holdings by *means other than transportation.*

With regard to labor practices, it is again true that shortsighted union demands have contributed to make feasible passenger runs into money losers. Yet, in some cases, management has been more shortsighted than labor. When diesel power made firemen superfluous, labor saw what was coming and bargained hard to keep firemen on the new trains. Management took diesel power less seriously, expecting it to be limited to a few high-speed routes, and so gave in to labor's demands. And while the railroads later got the firemen eliminated from the cab of most freight locomotives, they have failed to fight for that reform on what they seem to consider the already moribund passenger trains.

What becomes evident in a study of railroad developments over the last few decades is that railroad management has consistently resisted change, held back on innovations, and has viewed new transportation developments as threats rather than opportunities. It has reacted like the carriagemakers who smugly scoffed at that transitory, noisy, and undependable invention, the motorcar, and who preferred to go down like the dinosaur rather than branch out into the automobile business. When trucks began to make inroads into railroads' freight business, the predominant response of railroad management was to fight them tooth and nail by lobbying for restrictive legislation—instead of adding supplementary truck operations to make their own freight operations more efficient. Now the railroads would love to go into the trucking business, but they probably won't be permitted, partly because of the not unrealistic suspicion that they would use this privilege not to improve transportation service, but to cripple independent truckers through a price war the railroads could afford but the truckers couldn't.

Further examples of this shortsightedness are easy to find. For years, railroads kept on cooling perishables by stopping at intervals to pour ice into the tops of the cars; they didn't switch to mechanical refrigeration until trucks ran circles around them. Railroads are currently taking pride in their new innovation, "piggyback" service, in which highway trailers and other containers can travel across long distances hitching rides on various railroads along the way. But this "new innovation" was first experimented with in the 1920s, and one reason it didn't get out of the railroad yards is that by the 1930s Pennsylvania and New York Central (who have since gotten together rather uneasily) insisted on each using containers that could not be interchanged with the other's. This forced other railroads to make a choice between the two systems, or to invest in duplicate facilities, or to forget about the whole thing. Not surprisingly, under Depression conditions, most of them took the last option, and the implementation of this "great new innovation" had to wait another twenty years.

It should, therefore, have come as no surprise that after twenty-five months of study prior to the merger of the Pennsylvania and the New York Central, the incompatibility of their two computer systems had been completely overlooked—making for some real problems.

One of the things the "piggyback" story illustrates is that railroads have failed to make one basic leap of imagination: They still tend to operate as if their competitors were not airlines, trucks, buses, and cars, but other railroads. They are reluctant to pool and coordinate operations, even when it is clearly to their economic advantage, or to eliminate wasteful duplication of services. Even though they are now permitted to cooperate in many ways, most railroad management is paralyzed by a fear that the beneficiary of streamlining operations might be *another railroad*. All too often it is a case of incompetent management fearing other incompetent management.

And so instead of facing modern transportation realities and coming up with imaginative ways of adapting to them, the typical answer of the railroads is to do away with passenger service and raise freight rates. I think there are a number of reasons for not permitting them to do this. First, there is a real need for railroad passenger service—especially on medium-distance runs between large cities. No one who has recently spent hours in a holding pattern over an airport in an attempt to get to a city a few land-hours away should question this need. Nor should anyone who has inched his way to an airport—or to his destination—by means of automotive crawl. The increasing congestion of our highways and airways between metropolitan centers makes it daily more evident that we need more than one kind of transportation to keep America on the move. We need all the kinds we can get—planes, autos, buses, *and* the railroads. The fact that the New York-Washington Metroliner, which is clean, comfortable, and serviced by courteous and pleasant people, and which cuts the train trip from four to two-and-a-half hours, has been practically sold out since its inception, is another evidence of the attractiveness of train travel when trains are convenient and well run. For many travelers, air travel has lost its novelty and, with it, some of its glamour. In the years to come, people will be looking more coolly at alternative forms of travel, making more realistic comparisons of the time, money, convenience, and comfort involved in the various ways of getting where they're going.

The need for a railroad network in times of national emergency, for such purposes as the movement of troops, is another reason for keeping railroad passenger service alive. And then there are the eccentrics like me. Who knows, there may even be more of us in years to come, if someone makes an effort to woo us instead of making us feel like the orphans of the rails.

Not only is there a clear *need* for the continuance of passenger service, railroads have a clear *duty* to provide it. It should be remembered that railroads still have a monopoly on much freight transportation, and that at their inception received substantial governmental assistance. The right of eminent domain was exercised in their behalf; land grants were received. In return for these and other benefits, railroads have a responsibility to provide services that are useful to people—as well as hogs.

This is not to make light of the real financial problems railroads face. More government subsidies, loans, or forms of tax relief should be made available. But the big change must come in the *minds* of railroad managements. Right now, their operations are a casebook in how to go broke—how to *not* succeed by trying hard *not* to succeed! Managements must turn their attention away from the search for ways to get out of the business of hauling passengers to the search for ways to make passenger service attractive and profitable. (There are, of course, some efficient and forward-looking railroad presidents—but not many; certainly less than in any other industry of the same size.)

I suppose that the managements of really well-run industries—such as petroleum, timber, and life insurance—could, in the next fifty years, succeed in making those industries unsuccessful, too, if they tried hard enough and took enough hints from the management of railroads over the past fifty years.

If railroad managements do not wake up and adapt their practices to the needs of the traveling public, there is really only one alternative. Undesirable as it is, as a last resort the only way to save the trains for the people will be to turn them over to the Government. Government-owned railroad service in a number of foreign countries (Japan, Britain, France, and others) is far superior to ours; if railroads operating on a private, profit basis can't make a go of it here, Government can and must.

(There is already some sentiment for this among influential members of the U.S. Senate.)

It shouldn't have to come to that. If railroad management can break out of thinking that [it] is trapped in the past and find ways to intelligently approach the problems of the present and future, mavericks like me—as well as the traveling public as a whole—will be well served.

## D

This chapter from John V. Lindsay's *The City* proves to us why so many American citizens are not concerned with the problems of the cities. His quotations may remind you of the country mouse in Aesop's fables who decided that he preferred the country to the city. Instead of writing, however, of how one is superior to the other, the student might argue that this attitude should change; or prove by observation of those about him that this attitude does persist; or, by viewing his own sector of a city, prove that this anti-city feeling has prevented the solution of problems affecting his immediate area. Either of these topics would make a good composition.

### The Root of the City's Ills[4]

IN ONE SENSE, we can trace all the problems of the American city back to a single starting point: we Americans don't like our cities very much.

That is, on the face of it, absurd. After all, more than three-fourths of us now live in cities, and more are flocking to them each year. We are told that the problems of our cities are receiving more attention in Washington, and scholarship has discovered a whole new field to master and doctor in urban studies.

Nonetheless, it is historically true: in the American psychology, the city has been a basically suspect institution, reeking of the corruption of Europe, totally lacking that sense of spaciousness and innocence of the frontier and the rural landscape.

I don't pretend to be a scholar on the history of the city in American life. But my thirteen years in public office, first as an officer of the U.S. Department of Justice, then as Congressman, and now as Mayor of the biggest city in America, have taught me all too well the fact that a strong

[4] John V. Lindsay, *The City* (New York: W. W. Norton and Co., Inc., 1969), pp. 50–60.

anti-urban attitude runs consistently through the mainstream of American thinking. Much of the drive behind the settlement of America was in reaction to the conditions in European industrial centers—and much of the rhetoric behind the basis of freedom in America was linked directly to the availability of land and the perfectibility of man outside the corrupt impulses of the city.

What has this to do with the predicament of the modern city? I think it has much to do with it. For the fact is that the United States, particularly the federal government, which has historically established our national priorities, has simply never really thought that the American city was "worthy" of improvement—at least not to the extent of expending any basic resources on it.

As a center of unhealthy, immoral, and depraved citizens, the city has seemed to many of our important and revered thinkers a condition to be avoided, not a problem to be solved. And it is also a fact that we *do* make public policy out of private prejudices, particularly when such prejudices run through the mainstream of American thought. What I suggest, then, is that at least part of the dilemma we find ourselves in is a product of a long heritage that has taught us to divorce the city from the purpose and hopes of the American experience. I think, too, that as we look at what has happened to the twentieth-century American city, we will see the shaping impulses of eighteenth- and nineteenth-century thinking on what did—and did not—happen.

Antipathy to the city predates the American experience. When industrialization drove the European working man into the major cities of that continent, books and pamphlets appeared attacking the city as a source of crime, corruption, filth, disease, vice, licentiousness, subversion, and high prices. . . .

This was not, of course, the only opinion on city life. Others maintained that the city was "the fireplace of civilization, whence light and heat radiated out into the cold dark world." And William Penn planned Philadelphia as "the holy city," carefully laid out so that each house would have the appearance [*sic*] of a country cottage to avoid the density and overcrowding that so characterized European cities.

Without question, however, the first major thinker to express a clear antipathy to the urban way of life was Thomas Jefferson. . . .

. . . "I think our governments will remain virtuous for centuries," he wrote James Madison in 1787, "as long as they are chiefly agricultural, and this will continue as long as there shall be vacant lands in any part of America. When they get piled upon one another, in large cities, as in Europe, they will become corrupt as in Europe."

.   .   .   .   .

This Jeffersonian theme was to remain an integral part of American tradition. Throughout the nineteenth century, as the explorations of America pushed farther outward, the new settlers sounded most like each other in their common celebration of freedom from city chains.

.   .   .   .   .

We even find the first hints that those who inhabit the cities are somehow less "American" than their rural counterparts. The suspicion arose early in America—an Ohio settler wrote, in 1815, that insulation from the "foreign commerce" which touched the life of the eastern city would help insure that the citizens of Ohio would be "more patriotic."

The point is that all this opinion goes beyond ill feeling; it suggests a strong national sense that encouragement and development of the city was to be in no sense a national priority—that our manifest destiny lay in the untouched lands to the west, in constant movement westward, and in maximum dispersion of land to as many people as possible.

In fact, that was national policy, reflected in most of our important laws. While federal influence was extended into that one aspect of city life that was deemed important to the nation at large—development of port and navigation facilities to expedite trade—the impulse of the country was toward expansion rather than an effort to ameliorate conditions in the big city.

Thus, the Northwest Ordinance of 1787—perhaps the first important declaration of national policy—explicitly encouraged migration into the Northwest Territory and provided grants of land and free public lands for schools. New York City, by contrast, did not begin a public-education system until 1842—and received, of course, no federal help at all. Similarly, the Homestead Act of 1862 was based on an assumption—supported by generations of American theory—that in the West could be found genuine opportunity and that the eastern-seaboard cities of the United States were simply hopeless conglomerations of vice and deprivation.

This belief accelerated after the Civil War, for a variety of reasons. For one thing, the first waves of immigration were being felt around the country, and the economically deprived conditions of the immigrants, largely from Ireland and Northern Europe, caused many in rural America to identify economic want with personal inferiority—a trend that has not exactly disappeared from our national thinking. Attacks on the un-American and criminal tendencies of the Irish, the Slavs, and every other ethnic group that arrived on America's shores were a steady part of national thinking, as were persistent efforts to bar any further migration of "undesirables" to our country.

Accompanying this trend was the start of important attacks on the whole economic structure of the American economy—a structure in which concentration of wealth and poverty were both identified as evils associated with the big city. We see this kind of thinking even in optimistic works about the city. Thus, writing of western cities at the start of the 1860's, Jessup Scott predicted happily: "A large influx of these laborers, though it may lower the average character of our people, will, it is hoped, in a greater degree, elevate theirs."

. . . . .

With the coming of rapid industrialization, all the results of investigations into city poverty and despair that we think of as recent findings were being reported—and each report served to confirm the beliefs of the Founding Fathers that the city was no place for a respectable American. Indeed, this opinion grew. We find evidence of it in 1890, when, at the New York constitutional convention, a delegate defended malapportionment on the ground that since the rural communities of New York were wiser, more virtuous, and more moral than the decadent city, their residents *should* receive disproportionate weight.

Whatever the speaking ability of this delegate, his point was picked up and endorsed all over the country. It is safe to say that in the years of maximum population growth of the cities—between 1890 and 1950—not a single city in the United States was fairly represented either in state legislatures or in the House of Representatives. (Since state legislatures draw the congressional boundaries, it is easy to see why a malapportioned state legislature slanted in favor of rural areas would draw congressional boundaries that favored rural areas.)

Now consider carefully what this meant. This sixty-year period was the time when basic social legislation was being shaped in every state legislature and in the Congress. It was the period during which the basic taxation policy of state and local governments was set down in New York; the first basic commitment was made by state and local governments to various social and economic policies such as unemployment insurance, workmen's compensation, and home relief; and the first fundamentally important steps were taken in the structuring of state aid to localities, including aid to education. And it included the two great eras of federal activism in social concerns—the Progressive Era and the New Deal.

Thus, in all that time, the cities of America were never given their proportional voice in the halls of legislative deliberation, and all the fundamental charters of priority were set up without their full participation. And the laws showed it. Educational-aid formulas, for example, were carefully written so that big cities gained no advantage from the size of their populations, and in fact *lost* aid because of the very fact that they were contributing most heavily to teach their own children. The same laws initiated, at least in New York, the tradition of taking from the city far more than the state returned, and even of recognizing the necessity of losing some money to pay for state administrative costs.

Is all this relevant only to past attitudes and past legislative history? I don't think so. The fact is that until today, this same basic belief—that our cities ought to be left to fend for themselves—is still a powerful element in our national tradition.

Consider more modern history. The most important housing act in the last twenty-five years was not the statute that provided for public housing; it was the statute that permitted the FHA to grant subsidized low-interest mortgages to Americans who want to purchase homes. More than anything else, this has made the suburban dream a reality. It has brought the vision of grass and trees and a place to play for the kids within the reach of millions of working Americans, and the consequences be damned. The impact of such legislation on the cities was not even considered—nor was the concept of making subsidized money available for neighborhood renovation in the city so that it might compete with the suburban pitch. Instead, in little more than a decade 800,000 white middle-income New Yorkers fled the city for the suburbs and were replaced by largely unskilled nonwhites who in many instances represented a further cost rather than an economic asset.

Consider, too, the National Defense Highways Act (that name, by the way, graphically reveals the mentality of the 1950's, when a bill could not be passed if it did not include "defense" somewhere in its title). Under this bill, the United States committed itself to building an interstate highway system, ostensibly to insure that people and missiles could be moved effectively in case of nuclear attack. In fact, the bill was a $60 billion program for building highways, predominantly between the inner city and suburban communities and largely at the expense of inner-city neighborhoods. More than a dozen years have passed since this bill became law and we still do not have a federal trust fund that offers significant federal financing for mass transit.

And it was not a hundred years ago but two years ago that a bill appropriating a small amount of federal money for rat control was literally laughed off the floor of the House of Representatives amid much levity about discrimination against country rats in favor of city rats.

What happened, I think, was not the direct result of a "the city is evil and therefore we will not help it" concept. It was more indirect, more subtle, the result of the kind of thinking that enabled us to spend billions of dollars in subsidies ostensibly to preserve the family farm while doing nothing about an effective program for jobs in the city; to recognize agriculture, veterans, small business, labor, commerce, and the American Indian as legitimate interests but create no Department of Urban Development until 1965; to so restrict money that meaningful federal aid is still not feasible.

In other words, I believe that through a subtle link, the world of urban America as a dark and desolate place undeserving of support or help has become fixed in the American consciousness. And we are paying for that attitude in our cities today.

## E

This author disagrees with other educators about the value of teaching reading comprehension, and who could better prove the worth of his arguments than you students, since many of you probably had these comprehension exercises or tests. Or you might want to discuss his idea of "quantity reading."

His ideas might also remind you of some other educational theory that you think is false, or perhaps you want to support one you think is really good. Your personal experience should enable you to write well on a subject of this kind.

## The Fallacy of Reading Comprehension Skills[5]

In the past fifty years the experts have defined reading as understanding of print rather than the ability to pronounce written words. For almost 4000 previous years reading meant the ability to translate the graphic symbols into sound. Today we have changed the philosophy of reading and describe the act as more than the skill of identifying written sounds, words, and phrases. Reading is judged in terms of "comprehension skills" rather than recognition skills.

The important difference between these two definitions is that one represents a skill that can be taught, that is, graded by an expert and transmitted to a pupil; the other describes a power which can neither be graded nor transmitted because it does not exist as a separate intellectual ability. Reading with understanding (let us call it "compre—reading") strongly resembles listening, for classroom purposes. No educator seriously believes that he can teach listening skills for understanding any subject regardless of its content. The biology teacher, for example, does not claim that he is teaching listening skills when he directs learnings concerning the organs and processes in food digestion orally. What his pupils learn are the facts of digestion, not listening skills.

Our failure to examine the differences between these two definitions of reading has led to a host of instructional confusions. Thus we imagine that the reading teacher is teaching reading when the pupil is learning the sounds of *pl, str,* and *ell,* and also when he is struggling to extract the thought of a phrase, sentence or paragraph. We rationalize that belief by pointing to the print on which pupils focus attention in both these activities. We delude ourselves further by inventing a technical term, developmental reading, to identify possible learnings from it. The very existence of that phrase has motivated a search for classroom practices to implement it. Yet, despite fifty years of research and experimentation, no successful program has been devised to substantiate that philosophy of reading. As we explore the bases for the recognition skills and reading comprehension factors below, we will understand the reason for that failure.

An examination of the essentials of reading as learning should indicate

[5] Isidore Levine, "The Fallacy of Reading Comprehension Skills," *Elementary English* (May, 1970), pp. 672–77.

how the pupil can use his textbooks effectively through the process of *quantity reading.*

Reading as word recognition is the ability to call out printed words regardless of the content and no matter what the level of understanding. Thus a child in the sixth grade of elementary school who has been taught to identify the sounds and combinations of the letters of the alphabet possesses the skill of reading. He can transfer that skill from subject to subject no matter how abstruse the content. In other words, the sixth grader can read the following selections with almost equal facility.

"The important chemical property of oxygen by which you identify it is 1) its solubility 2) its color 3) its reaction with metals 4) its ability to support combustion." (from an applied chemistry test)

"The morpheme has figured in American linguistics along with the phoneme as a basic unit of analysis. It is perhaps most commonly characterized as a minimal sequence of phonemes which has a meaning, or, negatively, as the smallest succession of phonemes which bears no phonetic semantic resemblance to any other sequence." (from "Essays in Linguistics" by J. H. Greenberg, Univ. of Chicago, 1957)

The pupil may falter when he comes to the unfamiliar words, *chemical, oxygen, solubility, combustion,* and *morpheme.* But if he is urged, he will produce sounds clearly resembling the conventional pronunciation of those terms. In fact, if he is challenged, he can transfer his reading skill to

"When that Aprille with hise shoures swote
The droghte of Marche hath perced to the roote"     and

"In Italia antiqua duo mures habitabant. Alter mus erat pauper et rure habitabat."

He may regard the strange combinations of letters as frustrating or humorous. But his confidence in the sounds of *when, that, hise, In, Italia, duo,* and *pauper,* will enable him to achieve *swote, droghte, habitabant,* and *habitabat.*

The first factor in the skill of reading is that it can be applied universally to all print using our alphabet. The second factor is that comprehension does not necessarily enter into the experience of word recognition. However, the most significant element in word recognition is its similarity to subject matter in that it can be analyzed into component learnings and taught to the 98% of the children who master them. No special intelligence is required for such learnings any more than is demanded for the more difficult skills of speech.

Linguists assure us that all children except the speech handicapped have solved the grammatical and syntactic complexities of our language, with no formal training, at the age of five. The youngster who learned to identify and verbalize the thousands of sights in his daily routines of living can easily apply that almost innate ability to develop recognition of 200 sight words, 26 alphabetic letters, and some few hundred word parts. The latter constitute the analytic items of reading formulated for teaching purposes. The three year old who developed the capacity to say "dog" on sight of that animal accomplished that articulatory feat only after innumerable oral experiments with human made sounds. He can do likewise with such language symbols as *cat, mother, ound, vei, ade, pre,* and the other word parts unfamiliar to him at first sight. What he requires is the sight of a quantity of written symbols proportionate to his experiences with vocal and auditory symbols.

We can conclude then that the skill of word recognition can be described in the following trio.

1. It can be applied to all print using our alphabet.
2. Understanding is not the essential factor in its development.
3. It can be analyzed into component learnings and perfected by a pupil under the guidance of a teacher.

These three factors *cannot* be duplicated in the so-called comprehension skills. The latter cannot be applied to all print, cannot be perfected, nor, in fact, do any of them exist to be taught and developed. If we continue to maintain the deception that there are such skills of comprehension, we will spend another fifty years accusing almost 40% of our school population of inability to read.

Let us examine some of these alleged reading comprehension skills. Most writers on reading list these among the skills of comprehension: comprehension of sentences, paragraphs, and larger units; vocabulary acquisition; reading critically and creatively; organizing and summarizing; applying appropriate reading rates; locating specific information; using parts of a book; understanding and using formulas and scientific symbols; gaining accurate information from graphic aids; drawing appropriate conclusions; and evaluating and applying data. Some authorities list hundreds of subskills. (vide "Reading Grades 7-8-9-" N.Y.C. Board of Education, 1955)

The skill most commonly thought vital to reading for comprehension is the ability to deduce the main idea and supporting details of a paragraph. Undoubtedly all teachers have developed such a power if it exists. Yet it is only the rare instructor who can transfer that mastery from paragraph to paragraph below with equal facility.

## Entropy and Equilibrium

"Attempts are sometimes made to interpret chemical equilibria in terms of effects on the energy of a molecular system, without reference to entropy. Consider, however, the relation of an equilibrium constant K at temperature Y to standard changes in relevant thermodynamic functions (energy U; enthalpy $H = U + pV$, where p is pressure and V is volume; and entropy S)." (from Journal of Chemical Education May 1964)

## Continuous Variation

"A variable x is said to vary continuously through an interval (a, b) when x starts with the value a and increases until it takes on the value of b in such m manner as to assume the value of every number between a and b in the order of their magnitudes. This may be illustrated geometrically as follows:"

(from "Differential and Integral Calculus" by W. Granville 1911)

"If some of the voltage from the bottom end of the coil is fed through a small variable capacitor (Cn), called a neutralizing capacitator, onto the grid of the tube, neutralization is achieved. The neutralizing capacitor controls the amount of voltage so fed to insure that it is just enough to neutralize that arising from the capacitance of the electrodes. Since this neutralizing voltage comes from the plate circuit this method is called plate neutralization."

(from "Elements of Radio" by A. and W. Marcus, Prentice-Hall)

## Genetic Relationships Among Languages

The establishment of valid hypotheses concerning genetic relationships among languages is a necessary preliminary to the systematic reconstruction of their historical development. The appropriate techniques cannot be applied to languages chosen at random but only if preliminary investigation has already indicated the likelihood of the success of such an enterprise. Correct hypotheses of relationship are also of very real significance to the archeologist, the physical anthropologist, the ethnologist, and the culture historian, even in those instances in which systematic linguistic reconstruction has not yet begun and may, indeed, in our present state of descriptive knowledge be of only limited feasibility (from "Essays in Linguistics" by Joseph Greenberg Univ. of Chi. 1957)

*Income Taxes*

"Limitation on allowable capital losses.—If line 9, Part I, shows a net loss, the loss shall be allowed as a deduction, only to the extent of the smaller of (1) line 11b (or line 9 if tax table is used), page 1, Form 1040 computed without capital gains (losses), or (2) $1000. The excess of such allowable loss over the lesser of items (1) and (2) above is called "capital loss carryover." Any such carryover loss may be carried forward indefinitely. Short-term losses and long-term losses are to be carried over by category. In computing the carryover, short-term losses must be considered first."

There is little question that the reading expert possessing a background of science study could select the major points of information in the science paragraphs. But such understandings cannot be traced to a specific reading skill. Rather, they are the result of experience with science materials, and specifically, chemistry, as far as the initial passage is concerned. The teacher of English who prides himself on having perfected all the skills of reading could examine that selection on "Entropy and Equilibrium" with dictionary and reference work for hours and come to no meaningful conclusions. In fact, a survey of the succeeding sections in the article would simply increase his confusion. On the other hand, the sentences on the subject of language would be clear to him, but such insights would be due to wide reading and discussion in linguistics rather than the capacity to unravel paragraph complexities. The reading specialist conversant with the intricacies of calculus might revel in the simplicities of the paragraph by William Granville. But he would hesitate to ascribe such pleasure to a score of 13 plus on a standardized reading test. We can conclude that the ability to select main ideas and supporting details in a paragraph is not a skill that can be developed and transferred from subject to subject. A grasp of the concepts and data in a body of knowledge is assured when one has perused thousands of paragraphs in that subject. This doctrine will be discussed in succeeding pages.

A second reading skill alleged to be vital to the understanding of print is the power to detect and increase vocabulary meanings. If this were a skill in terms of the three criteria indicated above, then every teacher should be able to apply it to the previously quoted paragraphs in the same way he applies the word recognition abilities he possesses. Few teachers, however, will claim that mastery of the term *entropy* will add to the consummate use of *continuous variation,* or that familiarity with *variable capacitor* will clarify the mysteries of *capital losses.* In fact it is possible that the biologist acquainted with thousands of words in the vocabulary of living things might be unfamiliar with the word *enthalpy*. Further, the definition of *entropy* given in the 1962 edition of the American College Dictionary as "a measure of the unavailable energy in a thermodynamic system commonly expressed in terms of its changes on an arbitrary scale, being zero for water at 32 degrees F." merely opens new unknowns to most teachers of the humanities. No matter what their achievement in vocabulary, language arts teachers would hesitate to claim a skill which would enable them to use correctly the vocabulary of chemistry or physics without a study of the science in question.

Specific classroom training in roots, prefixes, suffixes, context-clues, connotations, multiple meanings, and dictionary usage may momentarily delight the teacher because of the intelligent responses of his pupils. But these periods of concentration on the vagaries of vocabulary cannot develop a non-existent word skill readily applicable to all print.

Another cardinal reading skill listed in textbooks on reading instruction is the ability to vary the rate of reading. It is claimed that pupils must be trained to scan some paragraphs but study others. Yet it should be quite evident that the reading teacher who is not a chemistry specialist can read the first selection above on entropy at 50 words a minute or 500 words a minute with no appreciable gain in understanding.

An individual's rate of reading is dependent on the proportion of unfamiliar words to familiar words in a selection. A fifth grader would read the passage on income taxes more rapidly than the one on languages because the number of multisyllabic unknown terms is much greater in the latter. However, regardless of his rate of reading in either passage, his comprehension of the paragraphs would be negligible.

We could examine every one of the remaining comprehension skills similarly and reveal the error of comparing them with word recognition as a reading power. None of them is a skill which can be mastered and then applied to all print. However, our purpose in analyzing these factors was not merely to expose the misconceptions they perpetrate. Our major concern was to offer a viable substitute for these erroneous theories of reading instruction.

## Reading for Ideas: Looking for a Subject 171

Only through quantity reading in a specific discipline will children gain knowledge and satisfaction in that area of learning. Quantity in this case means silent reading of a minimum of 3000 words daily in each subject to be studied. As the child pores over the thousands of sentences and paragraphs in novels or general science texts his eye and mind will become accustomed to the peculiarities of print language with its punctuation, capitalization, word order and technical terminology. In other words, the pupil will have developed the habit of reading for knowledge.

The rewards of quantity reading become obvious when compared with the results of quantity speech. Through quantity speech the youngster develops the far more difficult art of communicating orally while mastering the grammatical complexities, word order, and 5000–10,000 vocabulary bank needed for such verbal intercourse. Quantity speech can be measured in the 10–15 million words the average child hears and/or speaks annually. Simple multiplication will reveal that the child experiences as many words in his pre-school speaking years as there are in the scores of volumes of the Encyclopoedia Britannica.

Authorities have found that the toddler is inactive verbally less than one hour of his waking day. If he speaks or hears a minimum of 50 words a minute, an abnormally slow rate, he would experience 3000 words an hour, 30,000 words in a 10 hour waking day, and over 10,000,000 words a year. This sheer quantity of oral-aural phrases and sentences will culminate in the proficient use of oral language by all children except the brain damaged.

When teachers provide opportunities for the youngster to read as many words as he speaks daily, they can look forward to his communicating in print with the same confidence as his parents did in anticipating his growth in speech. Yet in the 400 years of formal education we have not varied the fundamental dependence on the spoken word as a means of conveying knowledge in the classroom.

In the elementary school today we spend three years teaching the child to read, that is, to recognize known words and articulate unknown words. When he has cultivated that skill, we assign him the practice of that power at home, instead of in school. Home reading assignments are least effective for those who need reading practice the most, the disadvantaged and the below average intelligence child. The latter two probably pass eyes over 100,000–200,000 words in the six years of elementary school. Compare that with the 60,000,000 words they hear and speak in the same period. The average child probably reads 600,000 to 1,000,000 words before he comes to the seventh grade, less than 2% of the number of words he articulates or audits. The superior reader peruses 2,000,000 to 5,000,000 words in the same period. Can there be serious doubts about the relationship between quantity of words read and mastery of the written language?

In the nineteenth century the reading experts stressed pronunciation and elocution as the goals of instruction in reading. No twentieth century authority would justify that philosophy today. However, the theories of reading comprehension skills are just as erroneous for the twentieth century child as were the principles of oratory for the nineteenth century youngster. When quantity reading is instituted in the classroom as the basic activity, teachers will have time for the individual attention each child needs daily. But the phenomenal change brought into the classroom when each child reads a few thousand words daily will be the creation of the habit of reading for information and recreation our knowledge explosion demands. The 21st century will demand quantity reading in the classroom.

# INDEX

*Androcles and the Lion,* 30–31
Appeals, kinds of, 63
  to emotion, 72
  to ethics, 67–71
  to reason, 63
  to senses, 19–20
Appositive, 32
Appropriate words, 24
Aristotle, 4–6, 98
*Art of Rhetoric,* 4
Audience, 11–13
Austen, Jane, 138
Authority, use of, 81–82
Avakian, Lindy, 37

Baldwin, James, 103, 147–154
Beagle, Peter S., 138
Black Hawk, 37, 73
Brown, H. Rap, 1
Burke, Edmund, 36, 49–50

Carson, Rachel, 39–41, 73–75
Chavez, Cesar, 7–10
Christensen, Francis, 38, 41
Cicero, 5–6
Circumstance, 81
Clause, 36–37
Cleaver, Eldridge, 34, 36, 39, 52, 55
Coleridge, Samuel Taylor, 23–24
Comparison, 80
Composition, body of, 105–109
  conclusion, 110
  ideas for (subjects), 140–141
  introduction, 101–103
  joining parts of, 115–116
Connotation, 15, 21, 23
Corax, 3

*Declaration of Independence,* 68–69
Definition, 79–80
Dialects, 12
*Die, Nigger, Die!,* 1
Discourse, ceremonial, 90
  deliberative, 93
  forensic, 91–92
Douglass, Frederick, 5, 104, 141–147
Drake, Jim, 7–10
Du Bois, W. E., 52, 83

*Ecclesiastes,* 16
Ellison, Ralph, 17–18, 38, 40–41
Emerson, Ralph Waldo, 13
Erasmus, 5–6, 24–25, 28–29, 84–85
Ethos, 63, 67–72
Euphemism, 23–24

*Federalist,* the, 5
Fischer, John, 121–129
Fleming, Ian, 39

Gilpin, Alfred, 93–95
Goodman, Paul, 69–70
Grahame, Kenneth, 22–23
Gregory, Dick, 71

Haiku, 42–43
Henry, Patrick, 72–73
Horace, 25

Indentation, 45
*Invisible Man, The,* 17–18
Isocrates, 3, 6

Jargon, 14
Jefferson, Thomas, 68

# INDEX

Kennedy, John Fitzgerald, 116–119, 136

L'Engle, Madeleine, 39–41
Levine, Isidore, 165–172
Levi-Strauss, Claude, 2
Lindsay, John V., 159–164
Logos, 63–67
Longinus, 33–34

Malcolm X, 34, 51, 55, 129–130
Mbiti, John, 19
Milton, John, 133
Multi-level sentence, 41–42

*New Yorker, The,* 35
Observation, 17–18
Orwell, George, 13–14, 16, 21

Paragraph, expansion of, 46–52
  indentation, 45
  topic sentence, 45–52
Pathos, 63, 72–77
Pellegrom, Daniel, 69
Plato, 3–4, 6
Poetry, *Abstractions,* 23
  *Afro-American Fragment,* 34
  *Fence, A,* 32
  Haiku, 42–43
  *New York Skyscrapers,* 19
  *Poor Man's Bees, The,* 111–113
Proposition, 4
Punctuation, 34, 36, 40, 42

Quintilian, 5–6, 98, 101, 105, 111–114

Relationship, 80
Revision, 136
Rhetoric, in Greece, 3–5, 13, 131
  history of, 3–5
  in Rome, 3, 5, 11, 131
Roper, Elmo, 154–159

Sandburg, Carl, 32
Schreiber, Servan, 32–33
Sensory appeals, 19–21
Sentences, balanced, 36
  compound, 36
  declarative, 30
  enumerative (appositive), 32–33
  expansion of, 38–43

indirect discourse, 31
interrogative, 31
multilevel, 41–42
patterns, 28, 34–35, 38
periodic, 38
punctuation of, 34, 36, 40, 42
repetition of patterns, 34–35
simple, 38
variation of, 34–35
Shiel, M. P., 137–138
Slogans, 15
Spender, Stephen, 104
Standard English, 12, 14
Stark, Freya, 25
Style, 131–139
  emotional, 135
  figurative language, 134–135
  high, 133–134
  middle, 134
  plain, 134
  revision for, 136

Testimony, 82, 107
Thesis statement, definition of, 54, 110
  formulation of, 56
  proposition, 54
Thoreau, Henry David, 17
Toomer, Jean, 35–36, 40, 138
Topics, 78–89
  common, 78–86, 107
  authority, 81–82
  circumstance, 81, 107
  comparison, 80, 107
  definition, 79–80, 107
  relationship, 80, 107
  special, 86–88, 108
  expedient (advantageous), 88–89
  moral (ethical), 88
Topic sentence, 45–52
Tuchman, Barbara, 43–44, 104

United Farm Workers, 7

Vietnam, 4, 35

Wald, George, 70
*Walden,* 17
Watanabe, Jiichi, 37
Words, 11–26
  appropriate–inappropriate, 24
  classification of, 25